ENDORSEMENTS

In the life-restoring ministry of Betel (described in these pages), we're always looking for modern storytellers, writers who can demystify ancient truths to make Scripture accessible to the hardest heart or most unbelieving 21st-century mind. *Fortify Your Soul* does that. It's non-threatening, easy and relaxed, like a coffee table book for the hungry soul, satisfying many tastes at once. It's a volume of personal letters, a thought-provoking journal, an inspiring devotional book, and a Bible study guide all in one. Forty sacred stories, all but forgotten by this generation, are retold with the crisp wit and seeming intimacy of a close friend who understands the disbelief of a "Christophobic" world. Laurie asks as many honest, jargon-free questions of the Bible as she answers. She cleverly draws out the pithy essence of these timeless accounts, simultaneously provoking a curiosity to understand them deeper—and the God who stars in them. How quickly can I get copies of this book for the hundreds of broken, recovering Betel men and women who need it?

KENT and MARY ALICE MARTIN
Directors, Betel UK

I have excitedly awaited the release of *Fortify Your Soul* by Laurie Hayden Bergey. Finally we have an excellent introductory book regarding the main characters of Scripture, written in easy-to-read language and accessible to all readers. This book is the kind that you need to buy a boxful and keep on hand for old friends and new believers. Laurie is a dear friend and someone I watched grow over the past decade, I wholeheartedly encourage you to check out this book.

JONATHAN WELTON
Best-selling Author
Director, The Welton Academy

I am delighted to hear of Laurie Hayden Bergey's fascinating book project and wish her every success.

REVEREND NICKY GUMBEL
The Alpha Program, Holy Trinity Brompton
London, United Kingdom

I am so impressed with this book. I can't wait to get it into the hands of patients and onto the shelves of the Caron Book Store. Laurie, keep in touch, and God bless your work.

"FATHER BILL" HULTBERG
OSFS Spiritual Advisor
Caron Treatment Centers

Working directly with the prison and recovery community, I would love to be able to pass *Fortify Your Soul* along just as we have the *Purpose Driven Life* by Rick Warren. *Fortify Your Soul* is very practical and easy to apply to the lives of those who wish to fulfill their purpose for the King of kings and Lord of lords, Jesus Christ. As we work with those who are continually struggling to find their real identity, this book will be another great tool to help them understand Scripture and the awesome plan that God has for their lives. Laurie Hayden Bergey has the full endorsement of Christian Life Prison & Recovery Ministries. We look forward to when she visits our ministry!

BOB SOFRONSKI, Executive Director
Christian Life Prison & Recovery Ministries
CLPRM.ORG

Fortify Your Soul is a creative and refreshing book. It brings three important strands together. First, stories: In today's world stories are what people love to hear and what better stories than Bible stories. Second, interaction: This book opens doors for discussion and personal evaluation. And third, purpose: The interesting thread of "40" takes readers on a journey that I believe will strengthen lives and activate destinies. Recommended reading!

STUART BELL, Senior Pastor
New Life Lincoln, England
Leader, Ground Level Network of Churches

Motivated by her strong faith and a deep love, Laurie began to write a series of letters to "Dear Dude" to entertain and encourage him as he was living through a very changing life experience. "Dude" told me that a group of his friends would gather around to hear him read the letters he received from Laurie. These thought-provoking letters were touching the lives of an unlikely group of people. I was honored to be there at the beginning to hear the first letters and am so excited to see them turned into a book that will touch many lives. *Fortify Your Soul* is a must-read!

PATRICIA L. CHAPMAN
Breeder/Owner of Smarty Jones
Kentucky Derby and Preakness winner, 2004

Fortify Your Soul is a refreshing look at 40 events in the Bible. The narrative is straightforward and true to the Scriptures. Laurie Hayden Bergey draws you in however, by painting the scenery around the story. Her observations introduce us to a Holy God with a sense of humor. I recommend this book for those who would like a fresh look at God's Word not just for the novelty but to help us think through how God wants to strengthen us. More than entertainment, Laurie's glimpses of God encourage you to love Him in return.

JOHN MANZANO
Leadership Director
Grace Presbytery

Fortify Your Soul provides a wonderful opportunity for some to begin a spiritual journey and for others to explore their faith and enrich their ability to manage life's challenges. I highly recommend this book to members of the recovery community who want to increase their knowledge of the role God can play in changing lives.

BEVERLY J. HABERLE
Executive Director, The Council of Southeast Pennsylvania, Inc.
Project Director, Pennsylvania Recovery Organization—
Achieving Community Together (PRO-ACT)

Without question, what comes to mind when I think of Laurie is patience, wisdom, and a discerning spirit. In her book *Fortify Your Soul*, you can for sure expect a reflection of these qualities in her narratives and helpful stories that will keep you pondering about God, life, and purpose. Laurie lives out what she expresses by "faith" on paper, helping those in most need and keeping many thinking about their life with Jesus. She not only lives out God's dream for her own life, but she echoes through empathy, and helps through genuine concern, the life expressions of many who ordinarily would give up, but instead move forward to a better future of hope and grace through Christ Jesus.

DAVID MICHAEL DONNANGELO
Author, *Dreaming God's Dreams*
Director, Kingdom's Keys Ministries

One of the things we love most about Laurie is her ability to reach people no matter where they are. This book is a necessity in everyone's collection because it will intrigue unbelievers to a level of desire that they never knew God put in their hearts, and it will spark hunger in believers, no matter what level their walk is, to seek God's Word even deeper. Laurie's compassion and love for all people truly exemplifies her walk with Christ, and we cannot wait for the book to come to print so we can share it with others!

Jerry and Teri Klinger
Redeeming Love Transformations Ministries

When a book excites you about reading the Bible, I say you have a winner! In this book Laurie has thrown a lifeline to the seeker *and* believer.

PAT HUBER, President
WBPH TV60

Fortify Your Soul is not like the Bible stories you might have heard at church. With her witty sense of humor and fresh, conversational style, Laurie Hayden Bergey shows you how God has changed the lives of people in the past and how He can change your life today.

JAMIE JANOSZ
Moody Bible Institute Professor
Author, *When Others Shuddered:
Eight Women Who Refused to Give Up*

Thank you to Laurie Hayden Bergey for writing an empowering, challenging, life-changing book that is so necessary. From my experience as a counseling psychologist, I can tell you that Christians and non-Christians alike are crying out to know their place in the world, wondering why life can be so hard, and what all this heartache is for. They want to change but need help to do so. *Fortify Your Soul* provides the structure to work through these challenges and will leave readers with a stronger sense of their own identity, potential, and greatness.

JENNIFER CRALL, PhD
Counseling Psychologist

Fortify Your Soul contains a refreshing narrative that is genuine, heartfelt and lovingly poignant. Laurie Hayden Bergey takes the truths of the Bible and makes them accessible and relevant to a post-modern generation by wearing her heart on her sleeve as she gives practical and powerful insights through a text that will draw you into the heart of our creator.

MICHAEL E. DUNSTAN
Youth Pastor, PNEUMA, New Covenant Christian

Fortify Your Soul is an excellent, well-written book addressing many of the issues and realities facing those who are incarcerated. I have used a number of different books and teachings in Northampton County Prison over the last 12 years and *Fortify Your Soul* provides the structure, hope, and answers needed, directly from the Bible in an easy to understand format.

CHAD LICSKO
Prison Ministry Leader
New Covenant Christian Community Church

These stories came to me at a time when I was questioning my being and worth. I was battling addiction, and many of the problems that come with that lifestyle. And, I had no faith. *Fortify Your Soul* gave me strength and something to believe in. Me! And now I give all the credit to God. I am well to this day and helping others in times of need. Laurie's knowledge and fun outlook on life make this book a "must read."

DAVID, the "Dude" to whom
Fortify Your Soul was originally written

FORTIFY YOUR SOUL

FORTIFY YOUR SOUL

40 LETTERS TO FRIENDS SEEKING PURPOSE AND PEACE

LAURIE HAYDEN BERGEY

Destiny Image Publishers, Inc.
P.O. Box 310
Shippensburg, PA 17257-0310
Promoting Inspired Lives

This book and all other Destiny Image and Destiny Image Fiction books are available at Christian bookstores and distributors worldwide.

Cover and Interior Design by: Terry Clifton

For more information on foreign distributors, call 717-532-3040.

Reach us on the Internet: www.destinyimage.com.

ISBN 13 TP: 978-0-7684-0601-6
ISBN 13 Ebook: 978-0-7684-0602-3

For Worldwide Distribution, Printed in the U.S.A.
1 2 3 4 5 6 7 8 / 18 17 16 15

DEDICATION

To my dudes, you inspire me!

ACKNOWLEDGMENTS

First I would like to acknowledge, well, of course, God! Lord, thanks for waiting for me all those years. I would truly be lost without You. You have been so faithful, patient, and generous. You have chosen better for me than I would have for myself, over and over again. You overwhelm me with goodness and mercy. You are a mind-boggling artist. I am in awe of Your creation. You are the highest standard for comedy and philosophy in the universe. Please protect me from putting You in a box. My desire is to know and love You well, and to help others to do the same.

Brook Bergey, my faithful and supportive husband, thank you for reading every chapter (over and over and over), and making what seems like a zillion useful suggestions. More than that, thank you for unlimited, unconditional love. You make me feel so loved, and so safe.

David Hayden, my super cool brother. Dude, you inspire me! I love the mug you gave me. "Be the change you wish to see in the world." You too! Oh, and thanks for saving my life in that crazy car crash back in our California days!

Ken Westgate, my safety net. I have stepped out on the tightrope a number of times. You have never let me "splat." I really truly appreciate you. Thanks for proofing the doctrine here! Thanks for extra encouragement when insecurity had me in a stall pattern.

Diane Wakeman and Lisa Rentler, thanks for your tips and pointers. I fear the editor will still have her hands quite full. It is not your fault!

Mom, what a wonderful place to proofread the final draft of this book. I'm sure most authors dream of escaping to an island or a secret garden to get away from life's distractions. Boca Grande is perfect for that! Plus, I loved getting to spend extra time tucked under your wing. Thank you, thank you, thank you!

To all my family, what a bunch of characters you are! Thank God! It has never been boring. Thank you all for being "there" for me always. I love my wild and wonderful family (not a family tree, more like a family forest).

Destiny Image, my favorite publishing company in the whole world, thank you so much for publishing this work. I am overwhelmed! The creative team was wonderful about working through so many of my unconventional ideas and special requests. I appreciate you!

Fortify - for-ti-fy [fawr-tuh-fahy] verb, -fied, -fy-ing.

1. to protect or strengthen against attack; surround or provide with defensive military works. 2. to furnish with a means of resisting force or standing strain or wear. 3. to make strong; impart strength or vigor. 4. to increase the effectiveness of, as by additional ingredients. 5. to strengthen mentally or morally: to be fortified by religious faith. 6. Nutrition. to add one or more ingredients to (a food) to increase its nutritional content. 7. to set up defensive works; erect fortifications.

Origin: 1400–50; late ME fortifien < MF fortifier < LL fortific?re, equiv. to L forti(s) strong + -fic?re -fy

I will sing, sing a new song I will sing, sing a new song I will sing, sing a new song I will sing, sing a new song.
—U2, Lyrics from "40" (Psalm 40 paraphrased)

CONTENTS

Foreword *by Tricia and Jack Groblewski* 21

Foreword *by Leif Hetland* 23

Introduction 25

An Approximate Time Line 29

PART I   Old Testament—Popular Stories Revisited 31

FORTIFICATION 1   Noah 33

FORTIFICATION 2   David's Early Years 41

FORTIFICATION 3   Jonah 47

FORTIFICATION 4   Moses 53

FORTIFICATION 5   Joseph 61

FORTIFICATION 6   Elijah 69

FORTIFICATION 7   Gideon 77

FORTIFICATION 8   David's Psalm 40 83

FORTIFICATION 9   Saul, David, Solomon 91

FORTIFICATION 10   Job 97

PART II   New Testament—From the Desert into Ministry 103

FORTIFICATION 11   Jesus in the Desert—Test One 105

FORTIFICATION 12   Jesus in the Desert—Test Two 111

FORTIFICATION 13   Jesus in the Desert—Test Three 117

FORTIFICATION 14   Andrew, Peter, John the Baptist 123

FORTIFICATION 15   Clean Leper 129

FORTIFICATION 16   He Healed Them All 133

PART III   Old Testament—From the Wilderness to Conquest 139

FORTIFICATION 17   The Ten Commandments 141

FORTIFICATION 18   Joshua 147

FORTIFICATION 19   Deborah and Barak 153

FORTIFICATION 20   Samson 159

PART IV   New Testament—On the Way to the Cross 167

FORTIFICATION 21   Loaves and Fish 169

FORTIFICATION 22   Calm the Storm 175

FORTIFICATION 23   Pharisees 181

FORTIFICATION 24   Two Blind Men 189

FORTIFICATION 25   The Greatest Commandment 197

FORTIFICATION 26   Lazarus 203

FORTIFICATION 27   Forty Minus One 209

PART V   Old Testament—Captivity and Restoration 217

FORTIFICATION 28   Joash 219

FORTIFICATION 29   Isaiah 225

FORTIFICATION 30   Jeremiah 231

FORTIFICATION 31   Nehemiah and Ezra 237

PART VI   New Testament—From the Cross to the Apostles 245

FORTIFICATION 32   Freedom 247

FORTIFICATION 33   The Great Commission 253

FORTIFICATION 34   The "Crippled" Beggar 261

FORTIFICATION 35   Stephen 267

FORTIFICATION 36   Saul Becomes Paul 273

FORTIFICATION 37   Philip 281

FORTIFICATION 38   Peter and Tabitha 287

FORTIFICATION 39   Cloud of Witnesses 293

PART VII Now—Your Turn 299

FORTIFICATION 40   "Chapter 40" 301

APPENDIX   140 Names of God 307

                      Recommended Resources 311

FOREWORD

D id you ever meet someone for the very first time and sense that you have come face to face with God-bundled creativity? That was exactly what we perceived upon meeting Laurie Hayden Bergey. Through our years of encountering her personality and her ministry, nothing has proven to be more evident to us as well as to our church than Laurie's ability to call into existence new dimensions of God's Kingdom! Laurie was creative before coming to Christ and in meeting her creative God she has discovered those artistic proclivities to be enriched and abounding. With her husband, Brook, they have pioneered a thriving jewelry business in which they create and craft the jewelry they sell. Their art is genuine. The jewelry is earthy and spiritual and beautiful and effortless and can aptly adorn anyone on any occasion.

We say this because now we have her marvelous book that follows this very suit. *Fortify Your Soul* sets itself apart in the world of spiritual literature. Provocative without being didactic or hyper-spiritual, we have a non-devotional devotional. It is conversational, witty, and its wisdom is accessible to a broad range of readers—spanning age and gender and life experience. And yet her letters never lose their spiritual punch. Bible teachers who are prone to pay attention to numbers in the Scriptures identify the number 40 as the number of testing. The children of Israel remained in the desert for 40 years. Jesus and Moses fasted for 40 days and nights. And of course there was the notorious 40 days of rain that launched Noah's ark.

Laurie has capitalized upon the notion that God uses those "40s" in the Scripture to take people to a new place. She envelops us in a "40" of our own, tailored to launch each of us into further development in His purposes and desires. Each of the 40 chapters (fortifications) in this book constitute an episode that develops into our own personal saga of growth in Christ. The chapters are based upon biblical episodes—but there is no "preachiness" here! The chapters are chatty and easy to read such that when we are challenged by her follow-up questions, we are disarmed and ready to discover something of ourselves as well as the God we serve.

Laurie's deep love and encounter with Christ explode into some of the more creative questions and provocations that we've encountered in this type of book. Her questions are not the usual devotional questions. For example, how many writers ask us to really consider whether free will was a mistake? But it is a great question. We laughed as we read it.

So get ready for an adventure! Whether you are 15 or 50—and especially if you are 40, you will have your spirit stirred as you travel through the many "40s" of this book.

But, a "pay attention" note to our fellow readers: Be wise and take time for full discovery. Listen for the Lord to speak to you. Honor the prophetic edge of the book. Let the Lord reveal what He wants to reveal to you. It will challenge and deepen your faith. But it will also delight your faith. You will enjoy the unique ways these stories have been written. Smile as you enjoy the fun and the personal quips. Let your imagination take you into your own world of God's revelation. This book lets you know that your author is really "real." She has lived, discovered, and gained wisely from God. You can too as you *Fortify Your Soul.*

TRICIA and JACK GROBLEWSKI
Senior Leaders of New Covenant Christian Community Church
Executive Director of Grace Presbytery Network of Churches

FOREWORD

I met Laurie and her husband, Brook, in a healing school I was teaching with Randy Clark and Bill Johnson. At the healing school, I spent many hours praying for Brook who was paralyzed as a result of an automobile accident.

Laurie wrote this book for a friend who was going through a recovery program. I was deeply impacted by the heart and passion of the author not only for her friend but also for anyone who has a need for a kiss from Daddy God. Laurie provides fresh bread for her friend and thereby provides fresh bread for each reader.

Selecting 40 as a number and love as a language, the author invites us on a journey that can transform our lives. It was December 2, 2005, when I arrived in Los Angeles, California, to enter a 28-day recovery program that led to five months of my life becoming what I call the "dark night of my soul." It would have been wonderful to have a friend like Laurie to dig into the gold mine of Scripture to encourage me at that time. It's been more than seven years since the season I call "the molting eagle." Only eagles that have been through severe difficulties know the value of providing fresh meat for an eagle alone in the wilderness. Laurie knows the helplessness and darkness that comes from facing crisis. She has experienced the fortification of heart, mind, body, and spirit.

Laurie has selected 40 invigorating revelations from many biblical characters who led "fortified" lives. She found that the one thing these characters had in common was trust. Trust starts by knowing God, believing in a God who believes in you. Laurie has made this personal! I believe that reading this book will upgrade your identity, dignity, and dreams.

For the next 40 days, take a journey and experience the life-changing power of God's Word manifested with the Holy Spirit giving revelation that leads to the glorification of Jesus. God will take you into supernatural new territory and your dreams will take you to your destiny.

LEIF HETLAND
President of Global Mission Awareness
Author, *Seeing Through Heaven's Eyes* and
Healing the Orphan Spirit

INTRODUCTION

One of the most precious people in my life called to tell me that he was heading off to a 28-day recovery program. He was going to be turning 40 during this period of time. I told this marvelous man that 40 is the perfect age to get his life together. It is never too late for a brand-new lease on life! I went on to explain that the number 40 shows up a lot in the Bible. We discussed a whole bunch of fabulous Bible stories that include the number 40. We couldn't stay on the phone forever, but he said he would like to hear more. I started to write my dear Dude a collection of letters.

This dear friend decided to stay at the recovery facility for an additional three months. I was glad to hear this, for two reasons: (1) he was being serious about his recovery, (2) I was having a great time writing him letters. Now I had extra time to keep writing. He was a "captive" audience! He had never heard the stories of the Bible put in such a way that they were interesting or relevant to him. He had always felt out of the loop, and that didn't bother him at all. But now something was different. "Dude" was loving these letters, and he actually gathered a group of people in the recovery program each time a new letter arrived. He read the letter out loud to a group of men, few of whom were normally interested in the Bible, and they would have a discussion on the topic of the letter.

This growing audience would call this time "Bible study." I was touched and amazed that this tough crowd was enjoying these letters. That really spurred me on. I thought it would be wonderful to end up with a collection of 40 letters based on the number 40. It is this completed collection of 40 letters, 40 stories written to my buddy that have been adapted into this book.

Now why on earth would that be interesting to anyone else? Because the biblical use of the number 40 is amazing, encouraging, refreshing, and fortifying. How many times do you hear the expression "40 days and 40 nights"? Which kings ruled for 40 years? Why 40? It is beyond coincidence that this number appears over and over! I discovered that when I encountered the number 40 in the Bible, there would often be an intriguing lesson. There was typically a time of trial with a relevant revelation and a positive outcome. As I studied the Bible to develop the 40 stories, I would come away with fresh thoughts and a renewed perspective. I discovered cool ideas and strategies that I could apply to my own life and share with others.

As I wrote about Noah, Jonah, King David, Peter, and many others being released to their assignments and destinies, paths would open so I could follow their testimonies to destinations of new beginnings, higher levels of victories, and heart-thriving revelations. This is what I shared in the "Dear Dude" letters. God loves us and He is excited about our fruitful destinies! God rocks!

These great Bible stories are told from my own perspective. They are recounted as a sister would casually tell them to a brother who has never really heard them, while eating chicken wings and pickles. The tone is informal and familiar. There are plenty of quirky jokes and inspiring insights. This is a voice that has clearly not been groomed by the Christian marketplace. For the book, I have added a section to each chapter that is meant to churn up questions, thoughts, and feelings. These contemplations will lead you to consider the content of the Bible more deeply, how it applies to life's circumstances. You will finish this book having a lot more information about Christianity. I suspect that *Fortify Your Soul* will make most readers hungrier for the things of God. Fortunately, there are many resources included to assist you in heading out on a path of discovery and adventure with God.

OK, ready? Roll up your sleeves, this could get messy (in a good way)!

AN APPROXIMATE TIME LINE

I'm including a time line because the stories in this book are *not* in chronological order. I will have you bouncing around within a 2,000-plus-year time frame. So, it will be beneficial for you to refer to this time line off and on and consider how all these chapters fit together in real time.

OLD TESTAMENT

- Adam and Eve: Some say 4000 BC, others say 60,000 BC, but really nobody knows. (This topic can start a fight...better just leave it alone.)
- Noah: Before 2500 BC
- Job: Maybe around 2000 BC
- Joseph rules Egypt: 1885 BC
- Moses leads slaves out of Egypt: 1446 BC
- Joshua enters Promised Land: 1406 BC
- Deborah is judge of Israel: 1209 BC
- Gideon is judge of Israel: 1162 BC
- Samson is judge of Israel: 1075 BC
- Saul becomes king of Israel: 1050 BC

- David becomes king of Israel: 1010 BC

- Solomon becomes king of Israel: 970 BC

- Elijah is prophet in Israel: 875 BC

- Joash becomes Judah's king: 835 BC

- Jonah is prophet: 793 BC

- Isaiah is prophet: 740 BC

- Jeremiah is prophet: 627 BC

- Nehemiah rebuilds Jerusalem wall: 445 BC

NEW TESTAMENT

- Jesus is born: When BC turns to AD (All these dates may be off a few years in either direction. I'm just simplifying.)

- Andrew and Peter join Jesus: 30 AD

- Lazarus raised from dead: 32 AD

- Jesus dies: 33 AD

- Stephen martyred: 35 AD

- Paul's conversion: 35 AD

PART I

OLD TESTAMENT—
POPULAR STORIES
REVISITED

NOAH

Hmmm…should I start with Noah? I don't want to scare you away with a forlorn flood and what might seem like an unhappy ending. Oh, but I must start here. Noah is the top of the Top 40! He is possibly the best known "40 story"; and this is the first time the number 40 is mentioned in the Bible. Think "40 days and 40 nights," and rain starts to fall in imaginations all over the world. Yes, we'll start with Noah. Grab a life jacket!

I think the story of Noah is awesome. But it is also sad. Basically, as we open this story, God is looking down upon the earth and He is disgusted by humankind. All He sees is evil. He looks to the left and sees evil, turns to the right and there's more evil. His heart is broken because when He made men and women, He made us "good."

Originally He had looked at humankind and He was proud of His craftsmanship, and He loved us. Along the way, we chose to listen to some strategic lies of the biggest liar of all time, and everything has broken down since then. (God allows us to choose Him, or not.) It sometimes amazes me that God didn't flush the whole human race right then and there. But God had something else in mind. He looked for something good, and He found something worth salvaging. He seems to like doing that.

In the days of Noah, when all God could see was that nobody had chosen Him, He looked again and noticed Noah. While God saw that the earth was like a sewer, filled with the filth of anger, violence, hatred, lies, and sickness everywhere, He also saw that Noah was a man of integrity. Sound moral rectitude, among other good qualities, saved Noah and his family (and ultimately humankind) from perishing in the great flood.

God instructed Noah to build an ark and to take his family on board. He was also instructed to take two of every kind of animal aboard with him. There would be a male and a female of each kind of animal, so they could repopulate the earth after the flood. They took extra (more than two) of certain birds, and the animals used for sacrificing to God.

Now consider this: Noah lived in a dry land, a place where it hardly ever rained, kind of like Arizona. It took him a very long time to build the ark. I've heard it took 120 years to build this super-sized boat. God was giving the people ample opportunity to choose Him. But instead of choosing God, people came from all around to laugh and jeer at Noah while he constructed this unbelievable mega-ship. I wonder if Noah ever wondered when the rain was going to begin. One hundred and twenty years! Did he ever doubt that he had heard God correctly? (I suspect that I would have doubted from time to time. Following through on short-term projects is hard enough!) Noah was probably encouraged when the animals started showing up. And, imagine his amazement when birds and animals that he had never seen or heard of began to arrive! Wow, what wonder and joy! I would have enjoyed that part of the ark experience.

Then, finally, down came the rain. The skies broke open and emptied all their water onto the earth. The water also came up from below, from underground springs. For 40 days and 40 nights, the water never stopped flowing. God washed the world clean with a flood. The whole earth was covered with water. Noah and his family floated high above the mountaintops for a very long time. I don't think the ark landed on a mountaintop for about a year. But you know what it is like to stand on saturated ground. You sink deep into goop. So, they could look at the land and long to get off the boat, yet they couldn't walk on the land for a long time. That must have been tough! Noah's family was locked tight in that boat. Ugh, can you imagine? After a week our family would be going nuts! Did I write a week? Hmmm…

Now on top of the family dynamics, think about this: Everyone else they knew was now dead. All their friends and extended family members died. But really…they had probably been among those mocking the ark and Noah the whole time anyway. Realizing the devastation, there must have been much tension and mourning in the ark. I would imagine that prior to the flood, Noah had tried to warn all the people about the coming danger so they could talk to God and be saved, too. After the flood, it must have been awful to know that they were the only humans left on the planet, a lonely responsibility. Eight people left to repopulate the whole earth.

Then one day something special happened, a symbolic moment. God put a big, fat, glorious rainbow in the sky. I love rainbows. I bet this was the best rainbow of all time. (Maybe it was a triple rainbow, and filled the whole sky!) God did this as a covenant with Noah. It was God's way of guaranteeing that He would never again destroy the world with a flood. That rainbow probably brought Noah and his family great peace. Without that colorful guarantee, imagine how they would think and feel the next time it started to rain! "Oh no, here comes another flood!" (Of course, the smart aleck part of me can think of many other ways for God to destroy the world other than by another flood.) The bigger point is that God would rather offer us a rainbow of reconciliation. Yes, God could destroy the planet. He's God! Instead, He chooses to offer us a brand-new day.

OK, still on the boat. Noah had approximately somewhere between 16,000 and 50,000 animals on the ark (nobody really knows for sure, it is not recorded), and the windows had to be shut for a long time.[1] It was probably hard to breathe in there, pee-yoo. Here is a sad fact: All the animals, insects, and even birds that didn't get on the ark were now dead, too. If there had been 1,000 elephants on earth, 998 were now drowned. If there had been 100 toucans, 98 of them were now dead. Bummer. I can't imagine that all the fish died though, since they can swim. Then again, was it freshwater or saltwater, and can fish switch from one to the other?

I don't totally understand this part of the Bible, why this happened to the animals. Humankind was supposed to take good care of (steward) the earth and the animals. When we made bad choices for ourselves, it affected geology and biology, too. But, this is not one of the topics I am going after today. I will still have many unanswered questions for God when I get to Heaven. Thank God I will have all of eternity to get them answered. Thank God that He is patient and kind. (YES!)

Part of the stuff we are supposed to learn here is that Noah heard God speak and followed God's leading, in obedience and trust. Noah built the ark and helped God preserve the human race. God gave the whole world a bath—a new start, a second chance. There was a new beginning. And that could, should, would have been a good thing, but...

Here is a verse from the Bible that is so weird that I am just going to put it in this chapter so you can see it with your very own eyeballs! This is what happened once they landed on dry ground. And so the new downward spiral began:

> *Noah, a farmer, was the first to plant a vineyard. He drank from its wine, got drunk, and passed out, naked in his tent* (Genesis 9:20 MSG—short for The Message, an easy-to-read translation of The Holy Bible).

New beginnings have all the potential to go well. Noah is a very good role model overall. But, he also had his faults. We must make every attempt to learn from Noah, and do even better than he did with the second chances given to us. We should always be prepared ahead of time for the next challenge. Since there is a potential to make mistakes, let's plan to have multiple strategies to avoid them.

––––––––––––––––– ∞ –––––––––––––––––

Each chapter ends with a few thoughts and questions to stir up your spirit, mind, and imagination. This section will probably raise more questions than it will answer. Be patient. Over the next 40 chapters, more and more questions will be answered, but not all of them. I have included many references—books, conferences, and websites where you can go for more information when you are finished with this book. These chapters should end up making you aware that there is a lot to think about Christianity and the Bible. In the end, you will probably find that you have an appetite to keep learning more about God. He is a God so big and amazing that He should easily hold our attention for the rest of our lives.

OK, here we go:

- When God was looking to the right and left and seeing nothing but evil, what types of behavior was He witnessing?

- How did that make God feel?

- Had He created humankind to be evil?

- What were God's original thoughts about the people He had created?

- What is "good"?

- Why would God give humans the free will to choose Him or not choose Him? Was that a mistake?

- How do *you* like having "free will"?

- Who is the biggest liar of all time?

- What had "broken down" since Adam and Eve chose to listen to this liar?

- Name some more works of evil you're likely to see in the daily news today.

- What are some differences between the times of Noah and the world right now?

- What is integrity? What is rectitude?

- Can you identify barriers to integrity in the world around you?

- How can you help to increase the level of integrity in your life and your environment? At home? At work? At school? With friends?

The Bible indicates that if you can be trusted with a little bit, generally speaking, you can be trusted with more. Noah's early years aren't recorded in the Bible.

- How do you think Noah started out?

- Do you feel like God just threw this assignment on him, or did God give him opportunities to grow into it?

- Do you think Noah had a choice? Could he have "passed" on building the ark?

- What are some of the things God would like to prepare you for?

- Are you afraid of being mocked for having faith in God?

- Would you like to contemplate God more, but you think people will make fun of you and block you?

- What are some ways to get to the other side of this difficulty?

- Are there other things blocking you from getting closer to God? Name some, and discuss how you can get past them.

- Is a clean new start a guarantee of a perfectly healthy new life?

- How can we increase our level of success when we start out on a new path? List some strong strategies for avoiding the downward spiral.

Your turn. Make up a few questions. What questions didn't I ask that you think would be interesting for thought and discussion? Tip: Avoid asking questions that can be answered with the words "yes" or "no."

In each chapter, think of extra questions. Write them down in case you work through this book with a group of people.

Note: This text has been influenced by Genesis, chapters 6 through 9.

ENDNOTE

1. *NIV Life Application Study Bible* (Tyndale House and Zondervan, 1988-2005), 19.

DAVID'S EARLY YEARS

David was just some kid who lived way out in the country. He was the youngest of eight brothers. The baby brother. His family raised sheep. David had to help as a shepherd. He would take his harp and go out to watch over the sheep. As a kid out in the fields, he would sing and write songs. One job of a shepherd is to make sure that the sheep don't get eaten by wolves and other wild animals. Another job is to move the sheep from pasture to pasture to make sure they are eating well. A third job is to pen them up for the night and let them out to pasture again in the morning. I suspect another part of the job is cleaning up messes. All of this, the shepherding and song writing, becomes important later. The shepherding because a king is like a shepherd to people. And the songs because many of the songs David writes are recorded as psalms in the Bible. In his early years, David built skills he used for the rest of his life.

There came a time, while David was still too young to defend his country, when his older brothers had to go off to battle. The enemy nation was called Philistine. The most dreaded warrior of the Philistines was a giant named Goliath who was awfully scary...and 9 feet tall. For 40 days Goliath stood in front of the Israelite army insulting God and threatening the people of Israel. It would go down like this: A one-on-one fight, winner takes all. One Israelite warrior would come up against Goliath. If he lost the battle, all of Israel would be subject to the Philistines, which was not good for Israel. By their standards, these people were barbaric. That's a lot of pressure to put on one man facing an armed giant. But if Israel would win, the Philistines would be subject to God's people. And ultimately, a victory for God's people is a victory for God.

I'm not sure how much David knew about what was going on. Even without TV and radio, he knew the general news, but probably not with perfect accuracy until he was on the scene, up close—"live." His father sent him to take food to his brothers at the battlefield. People joke that David was just the kid carrying the boxed lunches. When he got there, he saw for himself how Goliath would insult God and threaten the Israelites. They were terrified and cowering.

David asked, "What is the prize for killing this guy? He's defying the army of the Living God!" David was outraged at Goliath, so he decided he was going to talk to Israel's King Saul. (When I read this story, I always imagine my kid brother, also named David, coming out of the woods at the age of 14, hair windblown and face blushed red from running around catching snakes all day.) David's older brother tries to stop him, "Like, Dude, this is sooo embarrassing." "Uh, excuse my kid brother," he may have whispered to those around. "Pssst, David, go away." Nudge. Smack. He probably also wanted to keep his kid-bro safe from harm; grab the lunch and send David home, far from the battle scene.

The "heart" of David is awesome. He is the favorite Bible character of many people, completely understandable! This countrified kid just marches up to the king and says, "I think I can take the giant!" David goes on to explain that he has killed lions and bears while he has been out in the pasture watching over the flocks of sheep. None of the trained soldiers are coming forth, so King Saul puts his very own armor on David, pats the teeny-bopper on the shoulders, gulps and says, "Go for it, kid."

Well, imagine a boy in a man's armor. David could hardly stand up. He's wobbling from side to side just trying to walk in a straight line. Thankfully he has the sense to know that he has a much better chance if he fights the giant in the same way he fought the lions and bears that tried to kill his sheep. He takes off the oversized armor, grabs his sling and a few smooth stones, and takes aim. He hits Goliath right smack in the head, kills him, and wins the battle for the whole nation. Simple as that! After 40 days of terror, the battle is won by the most unlikely guy hanging around the battlefield.

And, over and over again through history, God has used some of the most unlikely people to shut down the enemy and deliver others to safety. Look for the least-qualified person for the job—and that person could possibly be the very one God chooses! God does not look at the things people look at. He doesn't look at outward appearances. The Lord looks at our hearts. He knows what is inside us.

THOUGHTS AND QUESTIONS FOR CONTEMPLATION AND DISCUSSION

God didn't choose an armed warrior to kill the giant; He chose a boy with a sling.

- Do you ever feel like you are "just some kid"?

- In what ways do you feel inadequate or less qualified than other people?

- What lessons did you learn as a kid that you are using now to fulfill your destiny?

- What are the similarities between being a shepherd and a king?

- How might some of the routine tasks in your current daily life be training you for greatness?

- Does the concept of "training for greatness" make you feel uncomfortable? Why or why not?

- What might David have been learning about God as he played his harp out in the fields?

- Do you sing songs to God? When and where? How does singing make you feel?

- If you don't sing to God, experiment with it. Make up a song about what is on your mind. Goofy, joyful, dark, or deep—it is all OK. Just try it. Sometimes I substitute more appropriate words into popular tunes that I like.

David used a sling to do battle and achieve victory.

- What is the "giant," the situation that is trying to threaten you these days?

- How have you gotten victory over giants in the past?

- How can you learn from the victories in your past, the victories of other people around you, and Bible stories?

- How can help like this shorten the time of pain and trial?

- What was the problem David had when he was dressed in Saul's armor?

- Are you trying to be someone you are not?

- Who are you?

- What are some unique skills and training you have that could alleviate the crisis at hand?

- Why do you think God so often chooses unlikely candidates to shut down our enemies and solve big problems?

- When it feels like God is giving you an assignment, what should be some of the first steps toward approaching and eventually completing the assignment? Because this is an early chapter, I'll give a few answers to this last question to get things rolling: Pray. Consult godly people. Read the Bible. Ask God for a strategy. What else? Make yourself accountable to other people. Go to healthy places. Form healthy friendships. Add at least five more things to this list. Don't be surprised if you use this list often!

The Lord looks at our hearts.

- What are some of the really special characteristics that God has put in your heart?

- What's in your heart? Believe it or not, this isn't the same question as the previous. This one is about your heart—personality, intuition, emotion, sympathy, feeling, affection, courage, compassion, enthusiasm, etc.

- Who are some of the people in your life? Let God look through your eyes and let Him show you some of the outstanding qualities He put in these people (whether you like them or not). Consider telling them some of the good things that you (and God) see in them. Maybe your encouragement is one of the keys that will open up their destiny!

Note: This text has been influenced by First Samuel, chapters 16 and 17.

JONAH

God spoke to Jonah. He said something like this: "I keep hearing stories about how terribly the people in Nineveh are behaving. Go and tell them I am going to blow them off the face of the earth." God is not the guy you want to upset. He holds the power of life and death in His hands.

Now for the part of this story you might miss, I am going to use USA geography. Maybe this will also bring the story closer to home. Imagine that Jonah is out west, maybe in Arizona or Colorado. God tells him to go to New York. Jonah takes off for California instead. Then he gets on a boat and heads toward China. God says go east; Jonah goes west; then he gets on a boat and goes even farther west. Obviously he doesn't want to take this message to New York. Even though he has clearly been told what to do, Jonah heads in the completely opposite direction. He is in direct disobedience to God. Make that double disobedience.

Meanwhile out on the boat, Jonah tells the crew members that he is running away from God. Lo and behold, a big storm comes upon the ship. The guys on the ship are from all different religions. They all cry out to their gods. Nothing happens. Waves are crashing on the ship, and everyone is in total panic. Jonah, believe it or not, is sleeping through the wild storm. The guys figure out that this storm is Jonah's fault and the only way to save the crew is to throw Jonah overboard. You have probably heard the next part. A huge fish swallows him whole and alive. Trapped in the consequences of his disobedience, Jonah prays that prayer…you know the one…the emergency prayer, "Oh God, if You can get me out of this, I'll do whatever You say!" Most people have said this prayer at some point in their lives, even people who don't believe in God! Some call this a "foxhole" prayer.

So this clever fish swims all the way around the United States of America (don't ask how, just go with it), stops right next to the Statue of Liberty, and spits Jonah out on the shore. Jonah wipes off the whale spit, yuck!, then looks up and sees the big green Statue of Liberty (there's some irony) and probably thinks something like, "Uh-oh, gotcha!" How often do people keep their "crisis commitments" to God? I'd guess it is maybe 50-50. Jonah wanders around for three days. NYC is huge, and he finally gets to Times Square. He summons the guts to yell to the crowd, "In forty days, God is going to blow this whole place to smithereens." (I like the word smithereens. Sounds like cartoon language.)

What happens next is totally unexpected. Everybody listens to him! Imagine that happening in Times Square! They look at how they have been living their lives. They cry out to God saying things like, "I'm so sorry. Forgive me." Or, "I don't even know what happened to my mind. This wasn't what I wanted to look like when I grew up. I had a dream. Lord, give me another chance." God looks down on them full of love and compassion and decides not to harm them. Instead, God blesses them with another chance to turn the whole thing around and make it all right.

I've seen billboards that say, "An educated person is familiar with the Bible." I went to the website of the folks who sponsor that billboard.[1] On this website, I read some articles about people who had not been given an opportunity to learn about the many ways that biblical wisdom has shaped our government and culture. Students who were interviewed by *Time Magazine* said they felt like they couldn't keep up in conversation; they felt "clueless," ignorant, and it bothered them.[2] They are like the people to whom Jonah was sent.

To discuss many important agendas of our day, or to stand firmly for or against something, it is beneficial to have at least a rudimentary understanding of God's thoughts on the subject. Jonah's crowd wanted to understand more than the cultural references that were used in a political speech, a book, a film, or a TV sitcom. They desired more than clever and informed conversation. When these people got an understanding of who God is, they wanted to dream again and fulfill the potential that was woven into their DNA by the omniscient God who had formed them in their mothers' wombs. There is a good reason why the Bible is the best-selling book of all time. Actually, it is the best-selling book year after year after year. It is influential, full of wisdom and grace. Some folks quip that B.I.B.L.E. stands for Basic Instructions Before Leaving Earth. It is the "users' manual" for the human condition! It is completely relevant.

I'd like to point out a quirky twist to this historical account of Jonah's mission to the Ninevites. Jonah doesn't particularly like the people to whom he was sent. After he delivers God's message, he goes off to a place where he can have a good view. He sits and waits for God to blow up the whole place. He's waiting for the fireworks! The big KA-BOOM! When he sees that God intends to show them mercy, he has a little tizzy fit with God. God explains to Jonah that it makes sense for Him to care about such a great city. After all, He loves people! We have one possible way of knowing that Jonah got over his big, ugly sulk. Jewish tradition holds that Jonah is the one who wrote this book of the Bible. He never would have confessed the tizzy fit if he hadn't made it right with God in the end. This "tiz" has been memorialized for our benefit.

Here's a special bonus, which just so happens to be another "40 verse." Jesus's burial and resurrection are compared to Jonah and the whale, big fish. In this way, Jonah is a type of Christ. Quite an honor.

For as Jonah was three days and three nights in the belly of a huge fish, so the Son of Man will be three days and three nights in the heart of the earth (Matthew 12:40).

THOUGHTS AND QUESTIONS FOR CONTEMPLATION AND DISCUSSION

- Does God speak to ordinary people like you and me, or does He only speak to people like pastors and prophets?

- What are some ways God expresses Himself to people, beyond using human words?

- Is it possible to run away from God? There should be an assortment of answers to this question depending on the circumstances. What do you think? Get creative with this one!

- Have you ever gone in the opposite direction from the direction that God is telling you, or the way you "know" you should go?

- Have you ever intentionally disobeyed God? What were some of the results of that experience(s)?

- Have you ever prayed the "Oh God, get me out of this one" prayer?

- What "crisis commitment" did you make with God at that time? Was it a deal that makes sense? Have you honored it?

- Does your life look like what you wanted it to look like when you were younger?

- Are there areas of your life that God would want to blow to smithereens because they seem far from His good plans for your life?

- What do you intend to do with these areas of your life now that you have heard that God is looking at you with love and compassion?

- There are some cities that God did blow to smithereens. What was different in Nineveh that made God change His mind?

- Have you ever been in a situation where you felt ignorant because you didn't know enough about the Bible? (I certainly have.)

- How did the Bible shape the U.S. Constitution?

- What percentage of the Bible references in films, political speeches, and in pop culture do you recognize or understand?

Start to consider how pervasive and influential the Bible is. Listen, look, pay attention. Desire to learn more. It is useful stuff. Even this book will lend a hand. But, if the Bible were a bucket of water, this book is merely a drop.

- Did you ever have to bring a message to a person or a group of people who make you uncomfortable?

- Have you ever met people who seem beyond the reach of God?

- Can you relate to Jonah's disappointment when the city didn't get destroyed?

- Explain why God would rather save than destroy this great city.

- Why would God send someone to take a message to people whom the person didn't even like?

- What areas of Jonah's character were improved through this experience?

- Why would Jonah write about his negative feelings of wanting God to blow these people to smithereens?

- How does Jonah use his tizzy fit to bring glory to God? What can we learn from that?

- What does it mean to be a type of Christ?

- What might three days in the belly of a fish have in common with Christ's burial, beyond the "three days" part?

Note: This text has been influenced by the book of Jonah.

ENDNOTES

1. www.bibleliteracy.org. I don't actually know much about this organization. I'm not sure if I can recommend their material, due to unfamiliarity, but I do like the billboards.

2. David Van Biema, "The Case for Teaching the Bible in Public School," *Time Magazine*, April 2, 2007, http://www .bibleliteracy.org/site/News/bibl_news070322TIMEMag.htm (accessed 4/28/14).

MOSES

Moses lived his first 40 years in the palace in Egypt as the adopted grandson of Pharaoh, the king of Egypt. At the age of 40, he had an identity crisis that changed his destiny. It became known to him that he was not an Egyptian, but a Hebrew. The Egyptians had been keeping the Jewish people enslaved for approximately 400 years. Moses's heart was awakened to their situation, and he wanted to see the Jewish people set free from slavery.

Being in such a close relationship with Pharaoh, Moses might have been positioned for great influence with the king. With the help of God, he might have been able to negotiate freedom for the slaves in a diplomatic way. But one day he went to watch the slaves working, to see how they lived. It broke his heart. He saw a slave driver hurting a Hebrew and got so upset that he wasn't thinking straight. Moses took matters into his own hands and acted rashly. He blew up and killed the slave driver. Oh, consequences! Moses ended up having to flee the country. He was officially a murderer at this point.

In the next phase of his life, Moses lived out in the wilderness, in exile for 40 years. It is there where God speaks to him through a burning bush. Moses is sent on an assignment from God to go back to Egypt and get the entire population of Hebrews out of slavery and deliver them to a special place God had promised to them. This "Promised Land" would eventually become the nation of Israel. Finally they would have their very own country.

You've probably seen the movie *The Ten Commandments,* the old one with Charlton Heston. (If you haven't, you should! It is a true American classic film! Epic! Plus, I'll be referring to it again.) This movie changes a bunch of stuff from what the Bible says, but I still love it. I can hear Charlton Heston, as Moses, bellowing, "Let my people go." In the Bible, Moses is very reluctant to take on this task from God. This is a huge assignment and he is really not up for it. God has to twist his arm, and ultimately Moses is yelling "UNCLE… UNCLE!" (Don't wrestle with God. He's bigger. You can debate, ask questions, and sometimes even bargain, that's all OK…but wrestling with God is just silly.)

Here's an interesting tidbit: Moses has some type of speech impediment. I'm serious. At least at this point in the history, Moses is assumed by some to be a stutterer, others think maybe he speaks like a foreigner, with a heavy accent and a reduced vocabulary. Either way, his brother Aaron does the talking for Moses a lot of the time. Can God use a stutterer, or someone with a foreign accent? You bet'cha. Big time! My opinion is that stuttering doesn't come from God. The enemy of our souls attempts to rob us of God's destiny and tries to use things like stuttering to shut us down or slow us down. When I get nervous, I sometimes stutter a little bit. It bugs me. This could make me hesitate to speak publicly. Moses was supposed to become a public speaker, a diplomat. The one who tries to rob our identity and destiny tried to block Moses from being used powerfully by God. It didn't work. God used him anyway. God is like that!

Next come the ten plagues on Egypt. Symbolically, these plagues dethrone the false gods of Egypt, and finally Pharaoh who is considered a god, too. After all the miraculous signs and wonders in

Egypt that eventually wore down Pharaoh enough to let the people go, Moses led the Israelites across the Red Sea. The water separated and a *huge* population (about two million!) of Israelites crossed on dry land. (It is fascinating to me that archaeologists today are still finding chariot parts when they excavate the Red Sea!)

On the other side of the Red Sea, the newly freed Israelites were probably only a few weeks journey away from the Promised Land. Unfortunately, there were some problems along the way. The biggest problem was that the Israelites had a bad attitude. They were complaining and griping nonstop. During this time, God was doing amazing things to provide for these whiners. The Lord Himself is traveling with them in a pillar of fire at night and a sparkling cloud of glory in the day. Think about it like this, count these blessings: (1) God's presence, (2) heat and light at night, (3) air conditioning for the hot desert days, (4) their clothing and shoes never wore out, (5) there was a rock that provided water! How illogical! (6) God-food called "manna" magically appeared right outside their tent doors every morning. It looks to me like one miracle after the next, but these people are complaining about eating the same ol' thing every day. So God even brings a flock of quail through, and they feast on meat for a few days. They want watermelon and onions. I'd want chocolate! "Oh God, send chocolate, how about some chocolate chip manna!" They started telling Moses that life was better in Egypt. Imagine thinking that slavery was better. Harsh labor? Whipping?

The Israelites are given a chance to send twelve spies into the Promised Land. It was a 40-day exploratory expedition. The spies come back saying, "Oh! No! Whoa! The enemies are so big and scary. They're giants. We are like little grasshoppers next to them." Out of the whole dispatch, only two brave guys (Joshua and Caleb) say that surely the Israelites should go in and take the land that God has given them. They point out that God is with them. But nope, they are over-ruled by the other ten. The Israelite nation chickens out.

At a certain point, God said, "That's enough! Fear? Bad attitude? No gratitude? No Promised Land! For forty years, one year for each of the forty days you explored the land, you will suffer for the sin of not trusting and relying on Me, and you'll know what it is like to have Me against you." The Israelites had to wander in the desert for 40 years. It should only have taken weeks. God told the Israelites that their children would be allowed to go into the Promised Land when they died, but not them. The first generation would have to wander for the rest of their lives. Eventually they'd stand on a hill and see the Promised Land, and then die. Can you imagine being the last person in that generation? All the kids would stare at you like vultures waiting for you to die so they can go into the Promised Land. "Bummer, Uncle Joe is still with us." If it were me, I'd be suspicious of every meal they brought me!

Kidding aside, I do feel bad for these folks. They spent 40 years walking in circles. They never arrived at their truest freedom. They'd only glimpse it from the outside, but it was right within arm's reach. How can you travel with a pillar of fire and eat miracle food every day, God providing you with one rescue and provision after the next, and not know that God is with you? They were ruled by fear, grumbling, and self-centeredness. Continually focusing on their problems kept them in a prison of sorts, wandering in an illusion that was so much worse than reality. They had brought it on themselves. How could they think Pharaoh (an image of satan) was better? God was ready to meet the desires of their hearts and all they could do was moan and groan. God is so good and His freedom is perfect, productive, peaceful, and profitable ($). What a shame to miss it!

THOUGHTS AND QUESTIONS FOR CONTEMPLATION AND DISCUSSION

Identity crisis.

- What is an identity crisis?

- Could you say that an identity crisis is when you are not living the life God had planned for you when He created you?

- Is it possible to have an identity crisis when you are living within God's plan? Don't just answer "yes or no," refine your range of answers.

Moses had a desire to abolish the slavery of the Israelites.

- How did his first attempt at this go?

- Did he use a godly technique to solve the problem?

- What happened as a consequence of taking matters into his own hands?

- Is being in exile a punishment, or a training ground, or _____? Dig around here; this might be deep.

- What if you feel like you might be getting an assignment from God, but it doesn't feel like it matches your personality and skill set?

- How can you discern if your feelings are correct or incorrect?

- How would you ask God for confirmation?

- What if it *is* your assignment, but it feels too big for you? What do you do? Where do you turn? What could be some steps to take toward developing new skills?

Investigate areas of your personality that have not yet matured.

- How can you start working on these things?

- Do you have to do it all at once?

- Why would God commission someone with a speech impediment to be a public speaker?

- What impediments do you have that seem to be blocking you from having a more fruitful life?

- How can you turn them into advantages?

- Are they things that can be changed?

- Can you use them to open doors of influence?

God likes to choose people who look unlikely for an assignment, just to show what people are capable of when they access God.

- Do you have any lifelong dreams that might actually be assignments from God?

- Have you ever seen a miracle?

- Is it possible for people to witness miracles and not believe in God?

- When people witness signs of God that make them certain God is near, why do they sometimes continue to exhibit negative thoughts, emotions, and behaviors?

- What would you miss most if you were stuck in the wilderness? Have fun with this one. (I would miss my computer and wireless Internet, and of course chocolate. Gah!)

Cultivate an attitude of gratitude. Make a list of things that you are grateful for. Do this regularly. Shout it out! Tell God about the things that are good in your life. You will find that the more you do this, the longer and longer your list will grow. You will find more things already in your life that you hadn't noticed. Then, as God sees your gratitude, new things will come your way, too.

Make a list of the negative attitudes mentioned in this Moses history.

- Are there any negative emotions that the Israelites had that you can identify with?

- How do these attitudes hinder you?

- Are you doing anything that might be blocking God from being able to move in your life?

- Which of these attitudes are you going to work on improving right this minute?

Many are hungry for freedom these days.

- What aspects of freedom in God are you hungry for?

- If you could have a little slice of Heaven in your life today, what heavenly things would you choose?

- How would you try to share them with the world around you?

Note: This text has been influenced by chapters in Exodus 2–4, 6–14, 16; Numbers 13–14, 32; Deuteronomy 8, 34.

ENDNOTE

1.   *The Ten Commandments,* Cecil B. DeMille, Paramount, 1956.

JOSEPH

In Genesis chapter 40, we find that Joseph is stuck in prison. His life wasn't supposed to go that way. He was his father's favorite kid, a good boy, and he was the one being trained to run the family business from the time when he was young. Dad had even made him his very own special cloak, all colorful and fancy, the original coat of many colors. Joseph's coat. His life was so glorious, it was almost like he was a little prince.

God also loved Joseph very much, and would talk to him in his dreams. These dreams made it clear to Joseph that he would rise to greatness. The big problems started when Joseph told his ten older brothers about these awesome dreams of greatness, and that he would be the boss of them one day. Dulp! Well, of course these brawling partiers got offended, and then they stuffed him into a deep pit in the ground. They were in the process of deciding how they were going to kill Joseph when a gypsy caravan came through. Instead of killing him, they decided to make some extra money by selling him as a slave to the gypsies who would in turn take him to Egypt and sell him to the Egyptians, never to be heard from again (they thought). Joseph might not survive, but at least the brothers would be innocent of murder, right? The brothers stole his fancy coat and covered it with blood. Then they told their dad that Joseph had been killed by a ferocious animal.

Once Joseph is in Egypt, he is bought by a pretty cool guy who sees that Joseph has been trained to read, write, balance a business checking account, and much more. It isn't long before this guy, Potiphar, puts Joseph in charge of running the whole estate. Potiphar is psyched because good help is hard to come by. Joseph works hard, and he is honest. By and by, Potiphar's wife checks out Joseph and thinks he might have something to offer her, too. She decides she'd like to get her hands on him. She tries to seduce Joseph…repeatedly. Joseph respects Potiphar and rejects the wife's advances every time. He always tried to avoid her. When she finally trapped and cornered him, he literally ran from her. Well, a woman spurned can be quite dangerous. She accuses Joseph of raping her. My personal opinion is that Potiphar knows it is a false accusation, but sadly Joseph gets thrown into prison for a very long time. I can't even imagine what a prison in those days would have been like. It must have seemed pretty hopeless.

Joseph is so smart and industrious that he figures he's not going to just rot there in the prison. Some folks do…but not him. He starts observing what he can learn, scoping out his options, and asking what he can do to help out. So, just like when he was a slave at Potiphar's estate, again Joseph is put in charge of running the prison bookkeeping and budget. He's still in prison, but he gets to exercise his skills instead of lying in a lump in the corner becoming vegetated.

After a number of years, Joseph ends up in the same cell with two guys who had been working for the Pharaoh. One was the cupbearer and the other was the baker. It had been discovered that someone was going to poison Pharaoh. Nobody knew who was behind the plot, so these two were thrown into the pokey. They each had strange dreams on the same night. Noticing that they seemed distant and preoccupied, Joseph asked if he could be of help. They told Joseph the dreams, and God told Joseph what the dreams meant. It turns out that the dreams cleared the cupbearer, but showed that the baker was guilty. The cupbearer was sent back to work at Pharaoh's side again. (A cupbearer is the guy who tastes the Pharaoh's food and drink to make sure it isn't poisoned. He is near the Pharaoh every time he eats. In other words, Joseph's old cell mate from prison was in an influential position! Funny how that kind of thing can happen.)

Over time, the Pharaoh started to have crazy dreams and nobody in the government could help Pharaoh understand what they meant, not even the official wizards. The cupbearer heard Pharaoh discussing this over dinner. He then remembered the help that Joseph had given him by interpreting his dreams. Now it was time to pay him back. The cupbearer recommended Joseph's skills to Pharaoh. Pharaoh invited Joseph to come out of prison and analyze his freaky dreams.

Joseph listened to Pharaoh very attentively; and then he prayed and asked God what was going on here. Joseph heard from God, then he told Pharaoh the meaning of the dream. In short, there would be a great famine that would affect the entire world. He also told Pharaoh the rest of what God had said, which included a download from God on how to store up food and prepare for the famine so that it would not affect Egypt. Actually, the plan would enable Egypt to help the whole world. It was a 14-year comprehensive plan. Pharaoh could plainly tell that Joseph was the right guy to put in charge of this entire enterprise, which was essentially running the country of Egypt. Joseph was immediately released from prison. Pharaoh handed him his credit card, went to CNN, CBS, and NBC (well all the media of the day anyway), and told them to spread the word that Joseph was now second-in-command over all the world. Joseph had passed all the tests put before him so far—pride, the pit, purity, productivity, and prison. No matter what kind of spoiled kid he had been, he had lived a challenging life as an adult. Through it all Joseph had proven to be a man of solid character.

It came to pass that the famine affected the entire known world… even Israel. Uh-oh, guess who was now starving? Yup, Joseph's ten older brothers, all their family members, and their animals. Ah-hah! Look who is in charge! Just like in the dreams when Joey was a kid; now it had all come true. The brothers would have to approach this man in Egypt who was in charge of all the food.

Joseph had a few more tests in front of him. How would he treat the guys who schemed to kill him, but then threw him into slavery instead? How would he handle his position of great power? Would Joseph be tempted to get even? What Joseph did was pretty cool.

His brothers did not recognize Joseph because he was dressed in the fancy wig and eye makeup of Egypt. Joseph put a few tests in front of his brothers to see if they had changed, and if they were capable of being good guys. Did they deserve a second chance? I guess you could say, Joseph was now the second most powerful man in the world. He could have done anything he wanted at this point. Joseph wondered how the group of brothers would behave if one of the brothers were taken into prison and held there. Would they stand by him or turn tail and run to protect themselves? As he watches them closely, he can tell that they have matured into decent men, men who deserved another chance. The brothers pass their test by keeping their word and standing together as a family.

In turn, Joseph also passed the rest of his tests—power, the palace, and pity (compassion). He embraces his brothers and identifies himself. It is a great family reunion. Joseph sends for the entire family; they were 70 people in all, plus the livestock. He has them all move to Egypt and settles them on the most fertile land, so they could run the family ranch. This is how the man named Israel (Joseph's dad), his twelve sons, and all their children came to live in Egypt. Four hundred years later they would amount to a huge population of people—descendants of Israel, the Israelites—all held in slavery in Egypt, but that's another story.

<hr>

THOUGHTS AND QUESTIONS FOR CONTEMPLATION AND DISCUSSION

God talked to Joseph in his dreams.

- Does this happen to you?

- Do you ever have dreams that you are sure mean something important?

- In what other ways does God communicate with you?

- What are some things that make you aware of God?

- What was wrong with the way Joseph shared his holy dreams?

- What was the family dynamic between Joseph and his brothers?

- Did his brothers have any right to get upset with him?

- How could they all have handled things differently?

We can learn much from how Joseph handled the crises in his life.

- How does Joseph handle slavery and imprisonment?

- How could he keep a good attitude when he'd been ripped off by life *so* badly? What can we gain from his example? Seriously, this is a good one! Slavery and prison are about as bad as it gets!

- How did Joseph discern the meaning of people's dreams?

- How significant were these dreams?

- How did God use this gifting to benefit Joseph?

- How did Joseph use this gifting to glorify God?

- Who are the people around you? How can you help them to look good at what they do?

Joseph learned the importance of serving God *and* the people around him. How did he show this? You know they say "actions speak louder than words."

- What was the training ground for Joseph to end up employed as "second in command" of the most powerful country in the world?

- How did Joseph treat Pharaoh? Did he simper or flatter him? Did he bargain with Pharaoh to be set free?

- What in Joseph's mannerisms and character must have attracted Pharaoh to give him such a powerful position right from prison?

The Bible says that Pharaoh could see the Spirit of God in Joseph.

- What did Pharaoh see?

- Is this something that people see in *you,* or that you wish people would see in you?

- What does (or should) "the Spirit of God" look like on a person?

- What must it have been like for Joseph to have his brothers come to him after all these years?

- What thoughts *might* have been crossing his mind? I give you permission to have some fun on this one...just for a moment.

- What is admirable about the way Joseph handled the situation with his brothers?

- What could be some risks of taking "testing people" too far?

- What is the difference between playing mind games and giving people a chance to demonstrate that they have changed?

Review the tests that Joseph passed—pride, the pit, purity, productivity, prison, power, the palace, and pity (compassion). These are common tests.

- Which have you passed?

- Which are your working on?

- What are you learning?

Note: This text has been influenced by Genesis, chapters 37, 39–47, 50.

ELIJAH

Elijah is one of my favorite Bible heroes. He did all kinds of cool stuff, like raise the dead, multiply food, and part water to cross a river. Elijah was a prophet of God, which pretty much means that God communicated with him in a plainly recognizable way. One of the most fascinating things about Elijah is that he didn't die. Instead, a chariot of fire and some heavenly horses appeared, separating Elijah from his buddy Elisha, then Elijah got caught up to Heaven in a whirlwind.[1]

His buddy Elisha became the next prophet. His story is twice as good as Elijah's, except that he dies. Elijah got a pretty slick deal here, skipping death 'n all. There are people who believe he still has some unfinished work on earth, and that is why he didn't die. (Maybe I'll write another book and tell you more about these guys. Their stories are too big for one chapter. This is just a slice of their pie.)

Once upon a time, Elijah had a powerhouse meeting with a group of false prophets. I say they are false prophets because they were prophets of the false gods Baal and Asherah. You probably have heard of Ahab and Jezebel. They were the king and queen of Israel at this time. They are also the leaders of "the bad guys" in this story. They had been killing all of God's prophets and promoting the false prophets into power. Elijah has heard that 100 of God's prophets have been hidden in caves so they wouldn't be slaughtered. But, there is Elijah, the only one left who has the courage to defend the name of God publicly.

Elijah refuses to go into hiding to preserve himself. He knows he serves the real God, and that they don't. He presents himself to King Ahab with a challenge for him, the false prophets, and the people of Israel during this dark age. He asks the people and the false prophets why they are wavering between the True God and other false gods. He says that because the Lord is God, the people should follow Him faithfully, not throw Him into a lump with all the non-God gods. (You can't have it both ways! God doesn't want to share you with false gods.) Everyone gathered will have to choose which side of the fence they are on. There is no neutral ground! Everyone sitting on the fence will perish with the bad guys.

There are like 850 false prophets gathered for the confrontation with Elijah. It goes down sort of like this: Each team will build an altar, sacrifice a bull, and the real God will "answer by fire" and burn the sacrifice. The Baals go first. They shout and dance and cry out and even cut their own flesh. Baal likes flowing blood. Baal still likes that flowing blood today, but it never gets his followers anything but pain and shame. Some people suggest that people who cut themselves are in a relationship with Baal and usually don't even know it. All they know is that cutting themselves brings some momentary relief. It never satisfies them, and they usually feel even worse later, a spiral of shame. There is freedom available to these people. (The name Jesus literally means "God saves.")

Anyway, the false prophets' altar never catches fire. Elijah has to bust on them saying, "Hey! Maybe Baal is busy, or sleeping, or traveling." Nothing happened for the Baals. No power, no fire.

Next, it is Elijah's turn to burn a fire on his altar. He has the false prophets pour water all over his altar, three times drenched. He throws twelve stones on the altar, too. The stones are a symbol of national unity for the sons of Israel. Elijah calls out to God asking Him to show the people of Israel that He, the God of Elijah, is the One True God. Elijah asks God to light the fire so that everyone in Israel will know that God wants their hearts to turn to Him, to burn for Him, as individuals and as a nation. Well, God shows up and the whole altar catches on furious fire and everything is completely burned up including the rocks and the water.

Elijah had an assignment from God, and God backed him up with a powerful miracle. The people in the crowd gave their hearts back to God that day. The false prophets were seized and slaughtered.

The same day, Elijah predicted a rainfall that would end a three-year drought and renew the land. He spent seven rounds of very intense prayer partnering with God to bring in this rainstorm. He never stopped praying until the rain clouds developed. Then the wind whipped up and a heavy rainfall came to finish off this very eventful day. So, you could say that Elijah had a great victory that day. But then (cue suspense music)...

When Jezebel found out what happened to all of her false prophets, she was furious and threatened to have Elijah killed. The thing I don't understand is why Elijah got scared and ran away. Why was he afraid after that great victory? This is a serious question! Elijah had just had a humungous confrontation with evil and more than 850 bad guys were overthrown. What happened to make him afraid of Jezebel, one woman? How could Elijah go from being so victorious to so fearful and discouraged? I have heard it suggested that Jezebel operated with a very powerful evil spirit. After all the excitement Elijah has just been through, he was exhausted. Elijah's batteries were running low. It was time to get recharged, to get with God. But Elijah wasn't sensitive to this need. He was too busy running away.

Next thing you know, he's out in the desert whining because he's all alone. He has decided he wants to die. An angel comes to him and brings him food. He rests, and then the angel feeds him a second time when he wakes up again. He now has the strength to travel 40 days and 40 nights until he comes to the Mountain of God. It is here that God comes and speaks to him in a gentle whisper. Elijah was complaining to the Lord that he worked so hard to serve God, and now all the other prophets are dead and there is a price on his head, too. The Lord assures Elijah that he is not alone. Many others (7,000) are waiting for him to come and get them.

God gave Elijah a list of things he would need to *go* and *do*. Now it is Elijah's job assignment to go back and do something to help. He will play a big part in calling out, educating, and activating these 7,000 people. He does this well. God also gave Elijah a special protégé buddy, Elisha, to hang out with and train. It is this Elisha who is at his side when he is taken up into Heaven in the whirlwind. Elisha goes on to do double the miracles that Elijah had done. A good mentor and prophet is proud to train protégés to go on to do twice as much as they have accomplished!

THOUGHTS AND QUESTIONS FOR CONTEMPLATION AND DISCUSSION

Let's think about prophets, gods, and idols.

- What is a false prophet?
- How can you tell a false prophet from a prophet of God?
- Do you know the difference between God and false gods?
- What is an idol?
- Why do you suppose it is so important to God that we clean our lives of idols and false gods, and don't listen to false prophets?

- Identify what might be some of the "false gods" and "idols" in your life.

- Do you put your trust in things other than God?

- What do you prioritize in front of God? Try making a list, and then challenging yourself to get rid of those false gods and idols. (Some of these things might actually be good things that have been elevated too high in your life, and just need to come into the right order.)

I think some people may read this book because they are considering choosing a "Higher Power."

- What should you look for in a Higher Power?

- Do you think and feel as if you are sometimes wrestling with powerful forces that seem to be in contradiction to what God wants for your life? There is a verse in the Bible that says, "If God is for us, who can be against us?" (Romans 8:31). Discuss the connection between the kind of power exhibited by Elijah and the kind of power that could be available to you.

Contemplate prayer and fear:

- How did Elijah pray to bring rainfall to the dry land?

- When it came to Round 6 and there was still no rain, what did Elijah do?

- What can we learn about persistent prayer and partnering with God in prayer from Elijah's example?

- Why did Elijah get scared and run from Jezebel? Is it that Elijah is worn down from the big event?

- Is there a source of power backing Jezebel? If so, what might it be?

- If Elijah were to look at the big picture, did he really have a reason to be afraid?

- What would have been some alternatives to the way Elijah handled this situation with Jezebel?

Fearful, discouraged, complaining, lonely, depressed, exhausted, maybe even suicidal.[2]

- Are you feeling any of the things on this list?

- Have you ever felt like you are the only one who is going through what you are going through? Like in Elijah's case, you're not. Start to imagine and discuss ways to cross to the other side of this season. P.S. Bible studies are great places to connect with people. You might even be able to use this book to start a discussion group. Discuss these questions, and add a few of your own! Hmmm...

- How did Elijah get to the other side of his depression? Name at least three things that helped to restore him to get back to his God-given mission.

Elijah was expecting something more like thunder, but God spoke to Elijah in a gentle whisper.

- In what ways can God speak to you? Try to name a lot of things!

- Are you listening and looking for God?

- When do you make time to listen and look for Him? Prayer is two-sided.

- Do you find that you run into people who are struggling with situations that are similar to problems that you have overcome?

- Why do you feel that happens?

- What do you do at times like this?

- How can you make sure these are opportunities to help others get closer to freedom and break free from their difficulties?

- What kind of relationship did Elijah have with God?

- In what ways was this relationship obvious to others?

- How were others affected by it?

Note: This text has been influenced by passages in First Kings 18–19.

ENDNOTES

1. 2 Kings 2:11.

2. A few resources for recovery, healing, and deliverance, just in case:

    - *The Supernatural Ways of Royalty: Discovering Your Rights and Privileges of Being a Son or Daughter of God* by Bill Johnson and Kris Vallotton (Shippensburg, PA: Destiny Image Publishers, 2006).

    - Randy Clark's Healing Schools, see globalawakening.com, or call toll free: 1-866-AWAKENING (866-292-5364).

    - *Heal Them All* by Cheryl Schang (Xulon Press, 2005).

    - "Father Loves You," a CD teaching on God's love by Leif Hetland. Visit: globalmissionawareness.com. (I heartily recommend all teachings by Leif Hetland. He has many books, CDs, DVDs.)

    - Caron Foundation, Comprehensive Drug & Alcohol Addiction Treatment Center; www.caron.org, or call the 24-hour hotline: 800-854-6023.

    - Teen Challenge provides care for adults and adolescents who need intensive help with life-controlling problems: www.teenchallengeusa.com.

    - Betel International is a great place to make a clean start. They have an amazing recovery record. They have programs and communities in more than 20 nations: http://betelinternational.org.

    - Alcoholics Anonymous at www.aa.org and Narcotics Anonymous at www.na.org.

GIDEON

I really get a kick out of the Gideon story. It is almost too goofy to believe. Well, that is unless you're the one going through it. Then it is very serious! Gideon is like the nerd hiding his face in his locker as the head ruffian walks by. The ruffians frequently assault him, punch him, and take his food and money. I've made it sound like a schoolroom drama, but this is actually a "life or death" scenario for Gideon.

Israel is being tormented by the Midianites. In general, these are people who follow Baal and other false gods, and they're fierce people, the ultimate ruffians. The Israelites are in hiding, living in caves and clefts in the rocks. The Midianites swarm their hiding places, senselessly kill their livestock, and ruin their crops.

Gideon is in hiding when "The Angel of the Lord" comes to him and says, "God is with you, O mighty warrior!" Gideon is like, "Yeah right...uh huh." Gideon thinks he is a nobody; and worse than that, he's a nobody shaking in his shoes hiding from the big, bad bullies. Imagine that was you and figure how weird it must be when an angel comes and talks to you. (Some say "the Angel of the Lord" is actually Jesus.) I'd imagine that has to get your attention. I wish that would happen to me!

Then Gideon asks a good and fair question, "If God is with us, why is everything so terrible?" The language switches. Now the Bible says the Lord (not the angel) answers Gideon saying something like, "I'm sending you. *You* are the answer to your problem."

Of course Gideon answers, "No way, I'm just a chicken nerd. In fact, everyone in my family is a chicken nerd, like for generations, and I'm the baby of the family!" The Lord says, "I am with you." Gideon asks the Lord to give him a sign that this is for real...and guess what—the Lord does give him a sign. That means Gideon is now on assignment, on a mission for God!

The first thing Gideon is instructed to do is cut down the altars to the false gods. This is a big deal. Very scary! He asks some friends to help him. They are so freaked out. Gideon and ten other guys go at night to cut down the altars. They actually use the wood from the false altars to make a killer bonfire, and cook up a bull, a sacrifice to God. Everyone in the town is stunned the following morning to see a new altar, built for the One True God. (I always wonder why nobody in town saw the big fat fire! I can't help myself. I tend to have extra-biblical quandaries. Not that I require answers, but I sure do have a lot of questions.)

Seeing the change of altars, this is when it gets the scariest. The Midianites join forces with the Amalekites, and the Mosquito-bites (Dulp! Dumb silly joke! There wasn't a nation, or even a tribe, in the Bible called the Mosquito-bites. Or was there? Nah...) With almost no choice but to stand up for themselves or die, Gideon blows a trumpet to gather the people for battle. He asks God for another sign. It is kind of weird. He puts a lamb skin (a fleece) on the ground and says, if the fleece is wet with dew but the ground is dry, then he'll be brave for the battle. It happens.

He's pretty sure he doesn't want to believe it just yet, so now he wants to double-check and asks God to switch it—wet ground, dry fleece. Once again, it happens. (By the way, this is a biblical model for asking God to confirm a big decision you have to make.) Anyway, it looks like the chicken nerd clan is going to have to stand up to the bullies. Now I have to clarify that they are not really "chicken nerds." They're a large family of people who feel powerless and are clearly outnumbered. These people are going to get a chance to stand up for themselves, with the help of their Almighty God. The nerd versus bully picture is just to get you to see how overpowered Gideon has been.

I don't know the exact number of bad guys. It could be maybe 300,000 or more. Gideon only had around 30,000 men. They are completely outnumbered. What happens next is just plain crazy. God actually tells Gideon that he has too many men. Huh? If Gideon's team would win, outnumbered 10 to 1, they still might think they did it in their own strength. So, God says to tell all the guys who are scared to go home. Holy moly, most of them are terrified, with good reason to be! After that, there are only 3,000 left. Now it is 100 to 1. Yikes! God says, "Nope, still too many. Get the guys to go down to the river and get a drink." Two thousand seven hundred men bend down and start lapping up water. Three hundred of them pull water up in their hands to their mouths, eyes sharp, looking around. God says, "Those three hundred are the men for the job. Send everyone else home."

Outnumbered 1,000 to 1, they do one of those surround-them-at-night sneak attacks. One of the guys in the enemy camp has a dream that Gideon wins the battle. He's telling his dream around the campfire. The bad guys are starting to get spooked. Hearing about that dream encourages Gideon and his men. These 300 men surround the enemy camp in the middle of the night waving torches, and blowing trumpets. As far as I can tell, that was all they did, except to also shout something about the "Sword of the Lord and of Gideon." My thinking is that God supernaturally scrambled the air-waves around the enemies, and threw them into confusion. The light of the waving torches, the sound of yelling and trumpets, and the echoing sound off the rocky terrain all worked together to freak out the bullies. Against all odds, these enemy guys started to fight their own men, killing their own team. The bad guys were all scattered and overthrown. This is a great victory for God, Gideon, Gideon's army, and Israel.

Maybe you're wondering, *Where's the 40?* Here it is: The people are so pleased with Gideon that they ask him to rule the country. Gideon says "No, God will rule the country." For the rest of his life, 40 more years, there is peace throughout the land. There are a number of morals to the story, but one of the big ones: If God can use Gideon, He can use anyone. When God is with you, you become the majority, even when you are weak and outnumbered. Another moral from this story: When God challenges you to do something huge, He'll help you get it done.

Now, "Git'er dun!" God is with you!

THOUGHTS AND QUESTIONS FOR CONTEMPLATION AND DISCUSSION

Unfortunately, many people today are shaking and hiding.

- How can it come to pass that someone God calls a "Mighty Warrior" is shaking in his shoes and living in hiding?

- Is shaking and hiding a reasonable response to the circumstances of Gideon's life (see paragraphs 1 and 2)?

- Would you say that Gideon has low self-esteem?

- Has this mindset ever affected you, or anyone you know?

Gideon asks, "If God is with us, why is everything so terrible?" There is a lot of evil in the world.

- Are things really as terrible as they may appear to be?

- What small steps can you take, as an individual or a group, toward raising hope and making changes in your sphere of influence? You may even want to start right away.

Gideon and a team start out by removing the altars to the false gods, and then build an altar to God.

- What would tearing down false altars look like in your thought life?

- What are some things you might accidentally consider more precious than God?

- What adjustments would you need to do to give God a more prominent place in your life?

- When God says, "I am with you," what does that mean? What are some of the implications of having God with you? Jesus said, "I am with you always" (Matthew 28:20).

- How can the Holy Spirit help us to overcome a scary enemy? Remember, Gideon seemed like an underdog, but he won the battle, even outnumbered 1000 to 1.

- How often do you underestimate what God wants to do in your life?

- How could you be the answer to at least some of your problems?

- Is it possible for someone who has lived under generations of oppression to be appointed as the leader of a revolution? Think of some examples in the Bible, in history, and maybe even in your surroundings.

There are places in the Bible where it clearly says that we are not supposed to "test God."

- Why is it OK when Gideon asks for a sign?

- What are some differences between attitudes of "testing God" and attitudes of "getting confirmation from God"?

- How is it possible to take "asking for a sign" too far?

The Word of the Lord, that is the Bible, is often called a "Sword."

- How does the Bible help people who are facing 1,000 to 1 odds win battles without having to fight a lot?

- Why do you think Gideon said "no" to the opportunity to become the ruler of Israel?

- Who did Gideon want to be the ruler?

- Why was Gideon's choice for a rule better?

- How can you apply that thought to your daily existence?

Note: This text has been influenced by Judges, chapters 6–8.

DAVID'S PSALM 40

After David killed Goliath, the giant, he became quite famous in Israel. He hung out with King Saul, played the harp for him, and wrote songs to God. They would also go into battle together. David was a great warrior. Then a big problem developed—King Saul became jealous of David, as the people of Israel would say, "Saul killed thousands, but David killed tens of thousands." Translate that: David is 10X better than Saul. Uh-oh! Saul turned green-eyed with jealousy. Saul became tormented by his love-hate thoughts, and an evil spirit to top it off. He was confused because he loved David so much, he hated David, he loved David—hate-love-hate!

Saul offered to marry David to his daughter. And then he tried to get David killed in battle. The price for the bride was 100 Philistine foreskins. Huh? Yup, that's what the Bible says. Good old David brought him 200 foreskins! Saul kept trying to get David killed in battle. But David was kickin' butt on the battlefield, and gaining even more popularity with the people. Eventually Saul ran David out of the country threatening to kill him. So David was on the run for many, many years, living in caves and hiding out. During this time he continued to write songs to God. Many of these are recorded as psalms in the Bible.

I couldn't believe it when I read Psalm 40. I thought about translating it into a 40 story, but it does the job by itself better than I could. It is cited at the end of this chapter. For now, I'll just give you the context of when it was written and describe some of how David thinks. David is in hiding from his enemies, and they want him dead. The neat thing about David is that he is so passionate with God, pure raw emotion. It is like his heart is naked when he talks to God. It is clear in Psalm 40 that he is feeling sort of abandoned by God, and it is clear that people are giving him a very hard time. He says, "I'm a mess. Make something of me. Don't put it off."

You can see his mood is half positive and half negative. He is trying to pray himself into a better mood. He's mostly successful, but he wavers. He latches onto God with all the strength he has left at the moment. He says he has read the Bible, God's love letter, and has understood how much he is loved by God. He is holding on for his life. "Hurry, get me help. People are mocking me." He says, "Your love and truth are the only things keeping me together right now." I know I am repeating what it says in Psalm 40, but it's such a perfect psalm for the "40" theme that you will see repeated through this book— coming out of the desert; surviving the flood; second chances; rescue and recovery; new life; starting fresh from today moving forward.

David stays in hiding for a really long time. One interesting thing that happens while he is in hiding, the "losers of society" flock to him. These are a bunch of guys who have nowhere else to go. Not technically all losers, they are predominantly outcasts, miscreants, and wanderers. David is their very last option. These people want to belong. They want to be part of something important, a cause, to back something they can believe in. David makes room for all of them. David takes this group of men and trains them to be "David's Mighty Men." There are only a few accounts of people killing giants in the Bible. All the others, other than Goliath, were killed by David's Mighty Men! Cool, huh?

I've heard the moral of the story is that if you want to kill giants, hang out with giant slayers and something will wear off on you as you learn how they do battle. I'd say another moral is that people can certainly go from being losers to Mighty Men and giant slayers. This text demonstrates that the most down-and-out people can become the closest and most trusted friends of the King. Once again, the future does not have to be defined by the past. Most of the Bible stories show how people screw things up, even royally, like King David will do in the next chapter. Then they make a comeback and do amazing things.

Psalm 40 is a song written by David to God. You might recognize the U2 song "40" in this text. That song is based on this psalm. Everywhere you see the words "He" and "You," David is referring to God. Here it is:

PSALM 40 (MSG)

I waited and waited and waited for God.
At last he looked; finally he listened.
He lifted me out of the ditch, pulled me from deep mud.
He stood me up on a solid rock to make sure I wouldn't slip.
He taught me how to sing the latest God-song,
a praise-song to our God.
More and more people are seeing this:
they enter the mystery, abandoning themselves to God.

Blessed are you who give yourselves over to God,
turn your backs on the world's "sure thing,"
ignore what the world worships;
the world's a huge stockpile of God-wonders
and God-thoughts.
Nothing and no one comes close to you!
I start talking about you, telling what I know,

and quickly run out of words.
Neither numbers nor words account for you.

Doing something for you, bringing something to you—
that's not what you're after.
Being religious, acting pious,
that's not what you're asking for.
You've opened my ears so I can listen.

So I answered, "I'm coming.
I read in your letter what you wrote about me,
And I'm coming to the party you're throwing for me."
That's when God's Word entered my life,
became part of my very being.

I've preached you to the whole congregation,
I've kept back nothing, God—you know that.
I didn't keep the news of your ways a secret,
didn't keep it to myself.
I told it all, how dependable you are, how thorough.
I didn't hold back pieces of love and truth for myself alone.
I told it all, let the congregation know the whole story.

Now God, don't hold out on me, don't hold back your passion.
Your love and truth are all that keeps me together.
When troubles ganged up on me,
a mob of sins past counting,
I was so swamped by guilt I couldn't see my way clear.
More guilt in my heart than hair on my head,
so heavy the guilt that my heart gave out.

Soften up, God, and intervene; hurry and get me some help,
so those who are trying to kidnap my soul
will be embarrassed and lose face,
so anyone who gets a kick out of making me miserable
will be heckled and disgraced,
so those who pray for my ruin will be
booed and jeered without mercy.

But all who are hunting for you—oh, let them sing and be happy.
Let those who know what you're all about,
tell the world you're great and not quitting.
And me? I'm a mess.
I'm nothing and have nothing:
make something of me.
You can do it;
you've got what it takes—
but God, don't put it off.

THOUGHTS AND QUESTIONS FOR CONTEMPLATION AND DISCUSSION

Go back to the beginning of the chapter.

- What is jealousy?

- How dangerous is it?

Try to identify areas of jealousy in your life and get rid of them.

- How can you get rid of jealousy?

- What is it, in general, that sparks jealousy in the first place? It is important to rip jealousy out from the roots so that you get rid of it completely.

David had a close relationship with God.

- How plainly and honestly does David talk with God?

- How do you think God feels about this type of openness and straight talk?

- Does it seem presumptuous or irreverent when David does this?

- How do you talk to God?

- What does David do with his bad mood?

- How is he feeling as he goes to God in Psalm 40?

- What do you think can happen when you take your problems to God?

- How might knowing the Word and character of God help in times of great vulnerability and need?

- Where did David's "mighty men" come from?

- Does someone's past have to define their future?

- How are these guys' lives transformed as they hang out with David?

- Why and how do you think that happened?

- Who do you identify with more, David or the Mighty Men? Why?

All the while that David was homeless and on the run, he was making a safe place for others to belong, and building an army. What can we learn from this? How can we apply this to our own lives?

In Psalm 40, David says he waited and waited for God. What does that mean? How long did he wait and what happened next?

Make a list of some "God-wonders" and "God-thoughts." Share these things with other people. Consider reading Psalm 40 in another translation of the Bible.

Think about verse 6. "Being religious, acting pious, that's not what you're (God) asking for."

- In this context, what does it mean to be "religious"? What would God prefer?

- How has reading and knowing God's words and thoughts affected David?

- How has it affected you?

- How often do you find yourself thinking about God's character and teachings? Have you noticed this increasing lately?

- What is guilt? Where does it come from?

- What does it feel like to get attacked by guilt?

- How can it be disabling in your life?

- What are practical and godly ways of dealing with guilt?

- Would you say that you are hunting for God? If yes, what did David put into Psalm 40, just for you?

- Look for his blessing in verses 16-17! What are you supposed to do with the blessing?

Note: This text has been influenced by passages in Psalm 40, 1 Samuel 18–19,24, 2 Samuel 22–23, and 1 Chronicles 11.

FORTIFICATION 9

SAUL, DAVID, SOLOMON

Saul was king for 40 years. During this time, David married King Saul's daughter. This wasn't the best marriage. She got really offended, downright angry, because David was out in the street dancing a mosh-wild-victory-praise dance to God. I think she ended up barren because of this. (God liked the mosh dance that had been done in His honor!) David had other wives, too (at least eight). My favorite of his wives is Abigail. David met her during the years when he was in hiding and Saul was trying to kill him. Abigail is smart and lovely in every way, a perfectly godly woman. If I were God, I would have made her an ancestor of Jesus. God had a different plan.

Check this out: King David has an affair with a married woman. (As if he didn't have enough wives; he had to go cheating!) She gets pregnant while her husband is away for several months at battle. David was actually supposed to be at the battlefield with this woman's husband. As you can see, King David is not where he is supposed to be. It will be clear to everyone that she had an affair. So David, now king, has it arranged for the husband to get killed on the battlefield. God calls this murder.

David then takes this woman to be his wife. Her name is Bath-sheba. You can remember her name because David first noticed her while she was taking a bath! He was up on the rooftop looking out over the kingdom, and voila, he sees a woman bathing. Oo-la-la, there is Bathsheba! But I digress... The baby David fathered with Bathsheba dies. Later they had another baby and named him Solomon. David promises Bathsheba that he will make Solomon next in line to be king when he dies.

David, Bathsheba, and their son, Solomon, are all ancestors of Jesus. When I first started to study the Bible, it surprised me how "messed up" Jesus's family tree is—prostitution, adultery, murder, false gods, and other impurity in his "great-great-grandparents." Just so you know, and this is kind of important, Jesus had what some might call a dysfunctional family. It's in The Book...the Bible. But it doesn't end there. The folks in Jesus's lineage typically seemed to pull it together with God's help, strange as their circumstances may have started out. (Hey! Looks like *we* aren't disqualified!)

David was king for 40 years, too, just like Saul. When David was about to die, his oldest son, who really was a bad seed, tried to take over the throne. Bathsheba came to David and said, "You promised that Solomon would be king." She held David to his word. And so it was. Solomon became king. And can you guess how long he reigned? Yup, 40 years.

Solomon was mostly a great king. There was peace and the greatest prosperity the nation of Israel would ever know during his reign. Do you want to know his secret to success? God came to him in a dream and told him to ask for whatever he wanted. Solomon asked for wisdom. Well, wisdom was certainly a good choice. Solomon had a great life. He was granted his request; and he was very wise in most things. So, remember to ask for wisdom if this "ask-for-anything-wish" scenario should ever happen to you!

Solomon knew he was young and the job in front of him would be overwhelming. Yup, he knew that he would need wisdom, so that is what he asked for. God liked his request and granted it to him. Consequently, Solomon knew how to run the government and make alliances, how to eat outrageously well and exercise, how to invest the kingdom's money, what to wear, what building was required, and how to decorate the palace. Great kings and queens would visit just to learn from Solomon. He was famous worldwide for the wisdom God had given him. Wisdom from God is different from the kind of knowledge received from school or a book. I had thought that this wisdom of Solomon's was mainly meant for politics and law. It turns out Solomon also had great wisdom in biology, fashion, and architecture. As a special bonus from God, Solomon also got to live his father David's greatest dream. He was allowed to build a great temple for God. It became known as Solomon's Temple.

See now, I really do wonder how wise Solomon was? Solomon most certainly had wisdom from God, but later in his life, he didn't always apply this godly wisdom to his personal or political life. Check this out. He had 700 wives of royal birth and 300 concubines. What on earth could he have been thinking? His downfall was that he married many foreign wives. The problem is that instead of them coming to know his awesome God, he let them build temples to false gods. His heart was swayed to confusion. The way in which he lived the latter part of his life became a bad influence for future generations.

I personally believe that Solomon got things right with God before he died, but his infidelity with God left a bad mark on the culture. There is a book in the Bible called Ecclesiastes. Solomon wrote this book, among hundreds or even thousands of other writings. He also wrote Proverbs, God's little book of one-liners. In Ecclesiastes, Solomon mentions that with unlimited wealth and power he tried pretty much everything. Solomon reports that through it all, though, the only thing that ever truly satisfied him was God. Out of all of his more than 1,000 writings, only Proverbs, Song of Songs, Psalm 72, and Ecclesiastes were included in the Bible.

THOUGHTS AND QUESTIONS FOR CONTEMPLATION AND DISCUSSION

When David did his mosh-wild dance in God's honor, he was breaking tradition. David was doing something new and pushing beyond the established boundaries of the status quo religion, and God liked it. God is not boring...and Christianity should not be stale and boring either!

- Can you think of something that you can do to honor God that might be new and outside of tradition?

- What do you think a "mosh-wild-victory-praise dance to God" might have looked like?

- Why do you think David's wife was offended by his dance? (See Second Samuel 6:12-16,20-23 for the whole story. It is pretty smooth reading.)

- What does it mean that David was not where he was supposed to be?

- What was he doing instead?

- What was the outcome?

Now, let's suppose that David and Bathsheba were divinely appointed to birth Solomon. Could it have happened without the adultery and murder? Explore these thoughts.

- Why would God have chosen Bathsheba instead of Abigail to be an ancestor to Jesus?

- How does it make you feel that Jesus had what we today call a "dysfunctional family"?

- God chose this lineage. Why would He do this? Why would He record it in the Bible? Was it really dysfunctional? That expression might offend some folks. That is not my intention. What do you think I was actually going for when I included that statement?

- If you could ask God for one thing, what would it be? Why? Why would wisdom be a good choice?

- What is wisdom? Is wisdom more than just accumulating information?

- What is the difference between being smart and being wise?

- Which aspects of wisdom recorded here give you a fresh perspective?

- What was the risk Solomon took in marrying wives from so many other cultures?

- What could have been some of the benefits of a king marrying daughters of royal birth from other cultures?

Ecclesiastes was written late in Solomon's life.

- Why would Solomon describe a long list of his experiences as being like "chasing after the wind" in this writing?

- What do you want to see when you look back at your life?

- Can you turn some of the yuckier moments from your past into something beneficial? Read Isaiah 61, a very, very, very short chapter, for more thoughts on this. Go deeper.

Note: This text has been influenced by passages within the following chapters of the Bible—Saul, Acts 13:21; David, 2 Samuel 5–6, 2 Samuel 11, 1 Samuel 25; Solomon, 1 Kings 1–4, 1 Kings 11, Ecclesiastes 1–2.

JOB

J ob's story is pretty crazy. (By the way, pronounce it "Jobe.") A bunch of angels went to visit God; satan went along, too. (I intentionally do not capitalized the "S." See copyright page.) God asked satan what he'd been up to lately. The devil said he'd been off roaming around the earth. He was out there setting traps for people, and when they'd mess up, satan would visit God and bring Him accusations of what these people had done wrong. (What a narc.) God asked the devil if he had checked out Job. It was a challenge of sorts. God bragged about how blameless and upright Job was.

The devil said, "If everything Job valued was destroyed, Job would curse You to Your face." God said, "I bet you're wrong. Go check it out." Poor Job—his job, his house, his family, everything got attacked by the devil. Job praised God through it all. God said to satan, "See, told ya so!"

Satan replied, "Yeah right, let me attack his flesh and bones, and then we'll see him fall." Poor Job got so sick, fever and vomiting. Plus, his whole body was covered in oozing boils. He was in extreme agony. Job's friends became totally annoying and were telling Job that he must deserve this calamity because "God had allowed it" to happen. What an awful support system, finding ways to heap blame on him!

(Please note: Blame is a devil tactic. It never fixes anything. It only divides people.) And then, even worse, Job's wife was telling him to "curse God and die." Wow! Yikes!

Absolutely everything falls apart for Job. Poor, pitiful Job has no frame of reference for what is going on. Job is the first book of the Bible to ever be written. So Job can't just pick up the Bible and read a story like, uh, Job. The written Word of God clearly shows us that the devil wants to test us, and destroy us, and then tempt us to curse God, too. Job ends up feeling very discouraged. He's been suffering, struggling, and not understanding why. He thinks God has most likely abandoned him. He has a lot of questions and no good answers. Job makes a list of all the things he has done right and why he shouldn't have to suffer. It is true that Job was a very good man, and he loved God. Even his thought life, his imagination, was morally pure.

Right about now a young guy rises up and starts telling Job useful stuff like this: It isn't about *you* and it isn't even about being a good man. It is about being a godly man. There *is* a difference! Doing good deeds can become a source of arrogance and pride. God's justice is pure and perfect. He gives you a heads-up when you are doing and thinking the wrong stuff. Make everything you do about God; the rest will fall into place. Keep your mind focused on how amazing and good God is. Then watch Him act on your behalf. But you have to partner with God by acting in obedience, being diligent, with a glad and grateful heart.

In Job chapter 40, God answers Job's questions, "Why me God? What did I ever do to deserve this?" The way God answers Job is to ask Job questions. These questions make it clear that Job is a man and God is *God*. He points out some great works of God, works of glory and splendor and might. Creation—strong cedar trees, raging rivers, thunder, hail, elephants, and crocodiles. The point God is making: "Who the heck are you to be questioning and challenging Me?" God doesn't actually owe us any explanations! He is always fair, and the works of evil are not from His hands. God is good all the time. Satan was testing a godly man. Job had to keep trusting God even when he didn't understand his circumstances. This was not easy, in fact it was torturous. Job stumbled through his terrible trials of legitimate loss and horrendous health with genuine grappling.

Job may not have understood his whole predicament and how it came to pass that he lost everything that was dear to him, right down to his own skin. What had Job done wrong? He spoke in ignorance, blamed God for leaving him, maybe he tried to be good in his own power (not relying on God). Maybe he was even a worrier and lived in a tension of fear that he would lose all that he held dear; there are strong hints of this possibility in the Job text.

But he did things right, too. He praised and worshiped God. He never cursed God, even on the hardest days. He admitted the things he did wrong and didn't do them again. And he apologized to God. He acknowledged that he wasn't in control, and that God was in control. Then he didn't wallow there in the mess. He started blessing his friends (even those annoying ones) and being the great man of character that he was created to be (the guy God knew Job was the whole time). God was able to show satan what an upright and blameless man looks like.

God actually blessed Job big time for passing this weird and terrible test. God gave Job double of everything that had been lost. God can more than make up for all the things and opportunities that have been lost. Blessing God and having a good attitude will go a long way in helping God take us to the other side of our circumstances! Job lived to be 140 and got to see his children's children to the fourth generation. His second shot at life was better than his first time around.

THOUGHTS AND QUESTIONS FOR CONTEMPLATION AND DISCUSSION

Some say that the devil can't visit God anymore, some say he can. Either way, do you think he is still sending bad reports about people to God? If he can't get there personally, are there other ways he might be able to "narc" on people?

- How do we (people) participate in this yuckiness?

- Do we sometimes act as the mouthpiece of satan when we talk to God, tattling on other people even in our prayers? (As if God doesn't know everything already!)

- Why would the devil have such a passion to see Job's life destroyed?

- How far-reaching is this destruction?

- How is Job feeling under the weight of all this destruction?

- Does he have a right to feel discouraged?

- What advantages do you have over Job for your times of tribulation?

- How about those friends who came to dig into what Job might have done to deserve this situation? Got any friends like that? Ever been that kind of friend?

- What are some differences between being a "good" person and a "godly" person?

- What were some ideas that Job's sensible friend had for shifting Job's circumstances?

- Can you still find things to be grateful for when it seems like everything is falling apart?

- How does God respond to Job?

- Is it fair to ask, "Why me, God?"

- Which attitudes are OK and which are not?

- Is it fair to blame God for diseases? Where do diseases come from?

The devil is a renegade terrorist on earth.

- How important is it to be aware of his strategies and tactics?

- What might be some dangers in spending too much time focusing on these things?

- How can you stay balanced?

- Where should you be fixing your affections and attention?

Review the things Job did wrong, and the things he did right.

- What can you take home with you from this lesson?

- What does it mean to be blameless and upright? How is this different from being perfect?

- How does God allow you to live blamelessly in relationship with Him?

- Was Job changed by this experience?

- What did Job lose, and what did he gain?

- How far-reaching was Job's restoration?

- How can you relate to any part of Job's experiences, restoration, and his relationship with God?

Note: This text has been influenced by the whole book of Job but concentrating more on chapters 1–3, 19, 33–36, and 38–42.

PART II

NEW TESTAMENT—
FROM THE DESERT
INTO MINISTRY

JESUS IN THE DESERT—TEST ONE

*Dear Reader, I want to remind you that the original version
of this book was written as letters to a very precious person in
my life while he was heading into a recovery program. This
particular chapter holds together best when left in that format.
You will see that the text addresses "Dude" specifically. Thank
you for allowing me the freedom to use the somewhat personalized
version of this letter instead of fully converting it into a "chapter."
Thanks for flowing with me now that I've explained the
context. You'll learn a smidgeon about Dude here. He's really
cool, a genuine tried-and-true fisher of men and women!*

Jesus was led by the Holy Spirit into the desert for 40 days where
He was tempted by the devil. This story is recorded in Luke 4 and
Matthew 4. It ends up being a very big 40 story. It also gets pretty
deep. I bet people have written whole books just on this section of
the Bible. I have to admit, this "story" is bigger than I realized before
I started writing about it. Therefore I'm breaking it into three parts,

three separate chapters. Actually, these three "Jesus in the Desert" stories will be a little more theological ("God logic") than storytelling.
After these three tests, I'll go back to the story format.

Let's get it clear right up front. These tests on Jesus are a very big
deal. If He had failed any one of them, He would have given in to
temptation. I once heard a really smart guy say, "It isn't temptation if it
isn't tempting." That means Jesus was very seriously tempted. Think of
how painful temptation can feel, almost like it is controlling your body
and will. In this case with Jesus in the desert, each test is not a single
temptation but actual layers of temptation. The easiest one to see and
understand is test one. Logically, we start there:

> The devil said to him, "If you are the Son of God, tell this
> stone to become bread." Jesus answered, "It is written: 'Man
> shall not live on bread alone'" (Luke 4:3-4).[1]

Jesus has been fasting. That means no food for forty days. His body
and will power are being tested here. He is hungry, that is the obvious
part of the test. His body is desperately crying out for food. But, for
God's very best outcome, He must say "no" and complete the fast.

This section also teaches us that more satisfying than any food we
could eat, the most satisfied we can be in life is when we are doing the
very thing that God created us to do. Maximizing our divine potential
is nourishing to the deepest part of our souls. Dude, just this morning
I started thinking about how much you love it when you hear there is a
new guy starting "detox." You practically run there elbowing and pushing everyone else out of the way because you want to be the first person
to greet him, tell him a joke, and make him feel welcome. I'm going to
guess that there is something in this that satisfies your heart in a way
that food or drink never will. Your compassion at that moment can
change a person's destiny, and something deep inside of you knows that.

Catch this: YOU were created in God's image. In a way, you extend
the caring compassion of God Himself when you go to that one person

who is breaking apart. When Jesus called His first two followers, He said to them something like, "You guys love to go fishing, but I am going to make you fishers of men...and that's much more wonderful." See, Jesus knew that their destiny was bigger than catching fish. He knew that they would be most fulfilled when they were saving men from drowning in their problems. I think you are a fisher of men. But, you may not know it just yet. I also bet a lot of the guys you are hanging with these days are fishers of men, too. Wait and see!

Some people say that the biggest test on Jesus right here is in response to the word "if" (also translated "since"). It is partly an identity test. Question: Is it possible that Jesus can be tempted to doubt that He is the Son of God? I believe it is. He was fully human while He was living on earth. If Jesus would have any element of doubt, the devil would try to inflate it. Additionally, the devil is probably mocking Jesus to try to manipulate Him. Furthermore, consider this: satan also wants to find out "IF" Jesus is the Son of God. Why? If Jesus is God, the devil is in trouble; it is "the beginning of the end" for him. If the devil can get Jesus to doubt His identity, it could be a sneaky way for satan to gain more power. It worked in the Garden of Eden. The snake (satan) was able to get Adam and Eve to doubt God.

This viper, the devil, is always trying to get people not to believe in God and His goodness. He wants us to extinguish our identity in God, our created value. Some of his top techniques are unbelief, hopelessness, and powerlessness. When you are feeling these things, the devil is hitting at your mind. He'll do it when you're in "the desert"—and he'll try it when you're in "the garden." He even does this to innocent little children. Don't let that happen to you. He is well-known as a liar, a thief, and a destroyer. But he has no power at all unless he can get you to agree with him. It's a battle in the mind, but it is a battle you can win. The value in understanding the Word of God is that you learn that God is for you and the devil is against you.

The devil accuses. Therefore, you want the best "lawyer" you can get. That is the Holy Spirit of God. Go back to the beginning of this section and note that Jesus has the Holy Spirit with Him. You may want to tell the Holy Spirit you need Him to be your lawyer! He knows the Judge, God. This might seem confusing, but the "Judge" and the "Lawyer" are actually the same Guy! The devil whispers to you that you're a loser, and bombards you with bad thoughts about yourself. God says, "I know every good thing about you. I made you that way. I have good plans for you. Follow Me. I'll help you get there. Talk to Me. I love you."

Jesus sets a really great role model for us here, in several ways; (1) He doesn't owe satan any explanation, so He doesn't offer one; (2) He doesn't give in to the temptation to prove Himself; (3) He doesn't give in to the temptation to satisfy His body when He is in a battle of discipline; (4) He uses the Bible to fight the enemy. Jesus's answer is straight out of the Bible. Check this out, it's cool:

The Word of God = His Word = 'S Word = Sword.

The Word of God is a Sword.

Isn't that awesome?!

The more you know about God and how good He is and how He designed each person for a purpose, the better equipped you are to beat the devil. The snake will come to you whispering dark thoughts into your head, even in your own voice, and he'll try to tempt you. Temptation isn't a sin. Don't feel guilty when you hear the whispering serpent. God is giving you all the ammunition you need for your next battle. The arsenal is loaded with great weapons and strategies. You are in a war, but we know who wins in the end. Be wise! You'll want to be on the right team.

THOUGHTS AND QUESTIONS FOR CONTEMPLATION AND DISCUSSION

Remember, temptation itself is not a sin.

- Who led Jesus into the desert?

- What happened there?

- What is temptation? Describe it.

- What is the source of temptation?

- Why is it important that Jesus not give in to temptation?

- When does temptation turn into sin?

- How can our compassion change someone else's destiny?

In John 4:34, Jesus said, "My food is to do the will of Him who sent me and to finish His work." How can it be possible that doing the thing that God created us to do would be more satisfying than eating food? I am inclined to make a chocolate joke here, but it really is a serious question. So, think about it, and answer it.

The devil is constantly trying to get people; (1) not to believe in God; (2) to doubt that God chooses us and loves us, and (3) to believe that God is mean, disappointed, and mad at us. How do you handle these battles? When this happens to you, it is a good idea to have multiple ways to get yourself to the other side of these mind battles as fast as you can.

Make a list of different ways to protect and defend yourself. I have found that talking to other people about what they do has increased my efficiency at handling this one. Sometimes I learn from people who seem unlikely, too. Keep an open mind, but use discernment.

How does the Holy Spirit help us? The Bible tells us that He is our Comforter and our Defender. He is also called the Spirit of Truth, Mediator, and Guide.

- What do these things mean?

- What does God say when the devil tries to convince us that we are ridiculous and we've made a fool of ourselves?

- What are the four things that Jesus did when this happened to Him?

- What are other techniques that you might have noticed but are not listed?

- How is the Word of God like a sword?

Note: This text has been influenced by Luke 4:1-4 and Matthew 4:1-4.

ENDNOTE

1. "Man does not live on bread alone" comes from Deuteronomy 8:1-3. This is part of another 40 story, Moses and the Ten Commandments with the Israelites.

JESUS IN THE DESERT—TEST TWO

The devil led him up to a high place and showed him in an instant all the kingdoms of the world. And he said to him, "I will give you all their authority and splendor; it has been given to me, and I can give it to anyone I want to. If you worship me, it will all be yours." Jesus answered, "It is written: 'Worship the Lord your God and serve him only'" (Luke 4:5-8).

We learn here that the devil has been given at least some level of authority over the planet Earth and Jesus wants it back. If you have ever wondered why the world is so evil, now you know. Christians are supposed to be "the body of Christ" and overcome the works of darkness in Jesus's likeness until He comes again. The problem is we aren't doing a good enough job of it just yet. I think it is because of ignorance. We, Christians that is, don't even understand how much power and influence we could/should have. Meanwhile, the devil is still lurking, and lying to everyone, and making it look like Christians are ridiculous and boring and set to ruin the party. Actually I have come to learn that there are some Christians who are doing an amazing job of being Christlike and reversing the works of the devil—and they are having a whole lot of fun, too. Those are the people I want to learn from.

Some history (His-story): satan started his life as an angel in Heaven. He was the most beautiful angel. He wrote songs to God and had the most amazing voice. (I wonder if he played a Stratocaster, or a Stradivarius? Of course there are those who say the devil only plays the accordion, or is it the banjo? Depends on who you ask!) Big problems began for him when he started thinking he was Mr. Thing. He decided he wanted not just to overthrow, but to displace and become God. He rounded up a whole gang of angels to be on his team. God kicked satan and all of his bad boy angel buddies out of Heaven. They were displaced to earth before earth was formed. Kicked out angels = fallen angels = demons. FYI: God's angels outnumber the demons 2 to 1 and are backed by, well, Almighty God Himself. The fallen angels are backed by satan, who is merely another fallen angel, nowhere near as powerful as his Creator.

When the Garden of Eden was created, the snake, the devil was there from the start. To keep it short, he lied to Adam and Eve. He got them to believe what he was saying and to doubt that God is always good and truthful. They consumed poison by giving in to the devil's lies, and eating the "apple." Out of ignorance and disobedience, they made an agreement with the devil that brought evil into all humankind. That is how satan got the authority mentioned in temptation test two (reread). So, the snake, the devil, is a liar and a thief. He has stolen our peace and our health. Oh, and blaming things on other people? That is another mark of the snake. Look at this, the first thing that happened in the Garden of Eden after they ate the apple was that Adam blamed the woman, and the woman blamed the snake, and the snake didn't have a leg to stand on. (No way! Was that a really bad joke or what!? It's actually not my joke, I'm just using it to lighten things up. And for what it is worth, a freaky little FYI, the snake probably *did* have legs at this point. He got punished by God for what he had done in the Garden of Eden. Part of the come-uppance for being a bad lizard is that he would have to crawl on his belly from then on. But I digress, again.)

Jesus has come on assignment to reclaim these earthly kingdoms from satan. The big problem is that Jesus would have to die, and even make a trip through hell, to complete His part of the assignment![1] For God to worship satan is just not part of the plan. But, I guess when Jesus saw all the kingdoms so twisted and smashed by the effects of evil, it broke His heart and He would have wanted to grab them out of the gnarled hands of the vile devil—instantly. I mean look around at children with cancer, and senior citizens lying dead and alone for weeks before anyone even notices they've died. Look at illness and poverty, oppression, slavery…. The list goes on: murder, theft, rape, violence, fear, lies, anxiety, addiction. This is the heart of this temptation. Jesus wants to eradicate these problems and see people set free. But it has to be done God's way. There will be no negotiating with the devil. He is the most ruthless terrorist in the universe.

Satan is an egomaniac and wants to be worshiped. He is not worthy of any worship at all. He is a cruel, false god. He wants to see all humans crushed, destroyed, and degraded. Why? Humankind is made in God's image. The devil wants to take all the God qualities out of humankind. He wants to conquer God and God's image. Good news: he'll never be able to conquer God. You see, satan is just a created being, created by God the Creator. We can trust in and be grateful for that.

In the meantime, God's people have to get serious and get educated. We have not been put here to judge or label "sinners," look down our noses at people, or act all goody-two-shoes, smug, and superior. Jesus was the only perfect Person to ever live. It is our job to help other people find peace and health. People can find ways to be proud of themselves and get happier, to prosper in jobs they like, where they can excel and make money. People can maintain fulfilling family lives and then go on to show other people how to do the same thing, and so on...until there is no more room on the earth for evil, sickness, sorrow, fear, mediocrity, complacency, discouragement, depression, etc. It is God's plan for people to lead much better lives, satisfied and fruitful.

Jesus wins this battle in the desert, but He also wins the bigger battle, because when He dies, He is raised again. Jesus plundered hell and walked out with the booty. He gets victory over death, and then hands the keys to the kingdom of Heaven to us. The same Holy Spirit who raised Jesus from the dead now lives in the "Christians" who believe that Jesus is who He says He is. That's a lot of power God gives to believers. We house resurrection life, and we need to understand what that means. Meanwhile, the devil still comes and tries to get us to agree with him instead of God. Don't listen. His lies are sugar-coated cyanide.

Jesus shut down devil test two by again quoting from the Bible: "It is written: 'Worship the Lord your God and serve Him only.'"

THOUGHTS AND QUESTIONS FOR CONTEMPLATION AND DISCUSSION

The Message Bible says, "Words kill, words give life; they're either poison or fruit—you choose" (Proverbs 18:21). Think about and discuss the harm that can be done just by the things we say, including "telling it like it is," sarcasm, and negative humor.

- How can we use our words to bring blessing and growth?
- What are some reasons why "the body of Christ," in general, might not be doing a better job of overcoming the works of darkness?

- How much power and influence do Christians have that they are not using?

- How has the devil tried to get you to doubt God? Maybe he gets you to think you are inadequate, or that God isn't listening, or even that there is no God, or that you are OK without God. Every person is likely to have a multilayered answer to this question. Dig for deeper layers.

- What are some strategies, works, and marks of the devil listed in this Fortification? Add to this list. Describe how the devil tries to attach himself to the way you think.

- Do you think there was a chance that Jesus might have agreed to worship satan?

- How likely is it that the devil would actually honor agreements he has made with people and God? Why did you answer this question the way you did?

- What is worship? Why does satan crave it so much?

- How do you feel about people worshiping you?

- Why is the devil so "hell-bent" on destroying all humans, even including preschoolers and fetuses?

- Why does he attack marriage and family?

- How can God's people help to overcome the works of darkness? Think of some simple things that you do, things that come easily to you, and you do them well. Then add things that seem too big for you to do without the help of God. Matthew 19:26 says, "Jesus looked at them and said, 'With man this is impossible, but with God all things are possible.'" How does this verse make you feel?

- Have you ever invited the Holy Spirit to live in you?

- What are some good reasons to want to house the Spirit of God? The same Spirit who raised Jesus from the dead can come live in you (see Romans 8:11). In quiet times, talk to God about going deeper with Him. Oh, and listen for Him to answer with words, whispers, and thoughts that are better than the ones you usually come up with on your own!

Note: This text has been influenced by these passages in the Bible—Luke 4:5-8; Matthew 4:8-10; Isaiah 14.

ENDNOTE

1.   This is according to the Apostles' Creed. This creed is a concise statement of belief made by the early Christian church, and adopted by many Christian denominations today. You can find this creed quite easily by doing an online search.

JESUS IN THE DESERT—TEST THREE

The devil led him (Jesus) *to Jerusalem and had him stand on the highest point of the temple. "If you are the Son of God," he said, "throw yourself down from here. For it is written: 'He will command his angels concerning you to guard you carefully; they will lift you up in their hands, so that you will not strike your foot against a stone.'" Jesus answered, "It is said: 'Do not put the Lord your God to the test'"* (Luke 4:9-12).

I have to confess, I'm pretty sure I'm missing part of this test. I've been thinking and praying over test three for a while now. Maybe you can tell me what's going on here. Think about it! Let's try to unpack these verses. Jesus is standing with the devil on top of the tallest building, a holy building. The devil says, "Do a swan dive and let's watch the angels swoop down and catch You. Do it, do it, do it! If David were here he'd do it. What, are you a girlie-man?" What is tempting about this? It would be a pretty cool air show if it worked. It could be a way for satan to find out "if" Jesus is the Promised One. It might be a temptation for Jesus to skip going to the cross if He starts flying around in the arms of angels, kind of like a super hero. Yet, if it doesn't work, Jesus goes splat, and that is that.

One thing I think is that maybe satan is trying to get Jesus to commit suicide. This supposition could ruffle some theological feathers, but in my little Laurie mind it bears consideration. I believe it is possible that Jesus could have died prematurely at this moment. Jesus lived on earth as a man. "Fully human, fully God" is a huge mystery to me; but someone who is fully human can be killed, generally speaking. One of Jesus's assignments was to be a role model, as a human who was in the right kind of relationship with God. He was actively training other people to do the same things that He was doing. Jesus was demonstrating what humans are able to do with the help of the Holy Spirit of God—heal the sick, raise the dead, mend the brokenhearted, set "the captives" free. All the devil knows for sure at this point is this Jesus guy looks like a threat to his plan to be intergalactic king. He's thinking, "I'm gonna git that pesky wabbit," a la Elmer Fudd.

Hey! Did you notice that the devil cites a Bible verse? Look at that. He says, "It is written," then quotes from Psalm 91. It's a nice psalm about God looking out for us and protecting us. Satan knows the Bible very well. The only time that the Word of God is a lie is when the devil is using it (on us and through us). Yuck. He's so rotten. It is like he has gone into God's arsenal and tries to use God's own weapons against God and His Son.

The devil actually *does* use the Bible against people. I've experienced it. In this case he is manipulating and changing the true meaning of the verse, misapplication. That's not a surprise. It is just another one of his evil devil tactics. This may be more of a trick than a temptation: To obey the Word of God when the Word is being wrongly applied. Catch this, it is very important: Jesus could tell that the Word had been twisted. He can spot the counterfeit because He knows the real thing so well. This is called discernment.

Here's another thought. There are definitely people who like to live on the edge, you know, bungee jumping, racing motorcycles, ice climbing, shark fishing, or even dating dangerous people. I wonder if Jesus was into extreme sports? Is this where the expression daredevil comes from? Is this a test of risk? Like driving 100 miles per hour? Is it like, "Nothing bad will happen. You won't get addicted. It's just an experiment. It'll be fun…an adventure…try it. Who knows? You might like it. You won't get hurt. That would never happen to you! Nope, no negative consequences will come from doing this really cool thing!" We can't take God's goodness and protection for granted. There are moments when we take our lives into our own hands. But our life is not ours to take. There is so much work to be done, so many problems in the world that need fixing, and we are the answers to many of them. To leave too soon robs the world of our intended value.

I don't know what every facet of this test means. It probably has a different meaning for each person who contemplates it. It could have been as simple as this: Testing God is dishonoring God. In any case, Jesus knows and shows us how to answer this temptation. For the third time, He uses a Bible verse to do battle. "Do not put the Lord your God to the test." I wonder, *Was Jesus speaking as God or for God when He said that?*

Look how this section ends. Jesus has completed this last round of testing and He has passed all of the tests in the desert. He proved Himself to have a pure spirit, soul, and body. But the ever-lurking devil has been waiting for thousands of years to overthrow God. He's not finished trying. The following Luke verse is creepy. The Matthew verse is more comforting.

*That completed the testing. The Devil retreated tempo-
rarily, lying in wait for another opportunity* (Luke 4:13
MSG).

*The Test was over. The Devil left. And in his place, angels!
Angels came and took care of Jesus' needs* (Matthew 4:11
MSG).

Wow, I've just had an afterthought: I just got a different glimpse
of this scene, a vision of sorts. I've always envisioned Jesus and the
devil all alone. And they probably were, but then again, maybe they
weren't. What if the angels mentioned in Luke 4:10 are standing there
ready to catch. There could have been a whole bunch of angels and
demons on the scene. In that case, there could have been some peer
pressure, jeering and taunting, showmanship, ego, "prove it" issues to
be dealt with, and so much more.

This desert test three goes a good deal deeper than this lovely little Laurie letter. In the end, Jesus passes the tests, and shows us how
to pass tests, too. But He is clearly weak and exhausted after these
40 days of fasting in the desert, plus dealing with that darned devil.
Trials, tests, and temptations can take a lot out of us.

THOUGHTS AND QUESTIONS FOR
CONTEMPLATION AND DISCUSSION

I'm convinced there is a lot more to this test than I have captured.

- When you read the Bible verses at the beginning of this
  chapter, what do you feel is the test? How does it relate to
  your personal life?

- Do you think it would have been possible for Jesus to die early
  and not complete the plan God had set before Him? Whether
  your answer is yes or no, develop this thought. Warning: Not

everyone will agree on this point! That's OK. We don't all have to agree about everything all the time.

- What is Jesus modeling? How is He doing it?

- Does the devil know and understand the Bible?

- For what purposes does satan quote from God's Word?

- How can we know the difference between a Bible verse coming from God-purposes and a Bible verse being manipulated by the devil?

About daredevils:

- Is it wrong to do extreme sports?

- What is the boundary line between taking our lives into our own hands in an appropriate way and in an inappropriate way?

- What can happen when we live too dangerously for too long?

- Is suicide testing God? Is it wrong? Is suicide murder? These are controversial and potentially painful questions, but they do bear contemplation.

- How would Jesus jumping have been putting God to the test? What would have been wrong about Him jumping?

- Go back and read Luke 4:13. How does this verse make you feel? What does it show you about the nature and practices of our enemy?

- Keeping in mind that it is "not in the Bible" directly, what do you think about the afterthought at the end of this chapter?

- Was there a risk that Jesus could have fallen for peer pressure, or given in to jeering, or putting on a show?

- Pressure and performance are genuine challenges in many of our lives. Do these tests influence your decisions and behaviors in any way?

- How does Jesus model His esteem for the Bible?

- Have you ever memorized a verse(s) from the Bible? As you go through this study, look up and memorize verses as you encounter chapters that fit the challenges and victories in your life.

Note: This text has been influenced by Luke 4:9-13 and Matthew 4:5-7,11.

ANDREW, PETER, JOHN THE BAPTIST

Andrew, Simon Peter's brother, was one of the two who heard what John had said and who had followed Jesus (John 1:40).

There was a guy called John the Baptist. Yup, that's right. He baptized people. He was drawing quite a lot of attention. People were thinking that He might be the Christ. He would hang out in the Jordan River and yell out, "Prepare the way for the Lord! Every tree that does not produce good fruit will be chopped down and thrown into the fire." The Jordan River is symbolic of life, and crossing into God's zone. You will see that Joshua and the Israelites crossed the Jordan River to enter the Promised Land. Another symbolism is this: As people go under water in baptism, it is like they are being born a second time. As the water breaks, a whole new life is starting. (Baptism humor includes plenty of jokes about holding people under water long enough to get the old way of life out of them. How long would that take, like until the bubbles stop? Thank God baptism is a supernatural exchange and we don't have to take it that far!) Baptism is also a prophetic act, a personal declaration that we are participating in a fresh start with God. God chose us, and we are choosing Him in return, washed clean, ready for a new life.

Anyway, John told people he was only setting the stage for the Christ. He said, "I baptize with water. The One who is coming will baptize with the Holy Spirit and fire!" In the fullness of time, Jesus went to check out John the Baptist. Well, John knew who He was right away and told Jesus that he felt silly baptizing the Messiah. John said, "You should baptize me." Nope, Jesus set an example for us and got baptized by John. When Jesus came out of the Jordan River after being baptized, the Holy Spirit landed on Him. Then They, Jesus and the Holy Spirit, headed out into the desert where Jesus stayed for 40 days, and was tested by the devil. After that, Jesus started His three-year assignment to represent (re-present) the exact nature and will of God, and to teach a group of followers how to overcome the works of the devil. These followers would learn to preach the Good News of God, heal the sick, raise the dead, cast out demons, cleanse the lepers, and mend the brokenhearted. They would do all this in the character of Jesus, and by the power of the Holy Spirit.

Let's back up a minute. Crowds were going down to the river to hang out and see what John the Baptist was doing. Some say that God had been relatively quiet for about 400 years when John came on the scene; so this was really exciting. Overt God-activity! Many people liked what John was saying. As a result, he had followers. One day, Jesus came to visit again. This was after the 40 days He spent in the desert. John saw Him and yelled out something like, "You see this Guy?! He is the whole reason I've been baptizing people. Everything I've been doing points to Him."

Two of John's followers took off after Jesus. They were literally walking along behind Him, following Him. Jesus turned around and asked them, "Waz up?" They gushed, asked Him all sorts of questions, and then hung out with Him all day and well into the night. When Jesus spoke, something came to life inside them. They couldn't explain it, but they had to stick close. As they hung on every one of His words, they felt excitement rise in their hearts. One of these guys is named Andrew.

Andrew's whole life was changed that day. He had met Jesus, and nothing would ever be the same again. Andrew goes to get his brother, Simon. Andrew tells him, "I have found the Messiah! The Christ!"

Simon goes with him to meet Jesus. Jesus looks at Simon and says, "I'm going to call you Peter the rock." A good while later, Jesus says to him, "You are Peter, and on this rock I will build my church, and the gates of Hades will not overcome it."[1] (It is interesting to note that many people say Peter was the first pope of the Catholic denomination.) Because Andrew met Jesus and knew without a doubt that this Man was the One to follow, and because Andrew was ready to share this revelation, his brother Peter came to know Jesus, too. That is kind of what I am doing with you. Then you can run right past me and go farther than me into the Kingdom, just like Peter did with Andrew. Go on, take a good look at yourself. You were born for this!

Andrew and Peter were both fishermen. Jesus came by as they were getting off work one day. They were exhausted and they hadn't caught a thing all night. Jesus jumped into the boat and taught some God-thoughts from the boat to some people who had gathered by the shore. After that He said, "Let's just put out a little bit off shore and cast the nets one more time."

The guys were like, "Come on! We're exhausted, Man! We just got off work. No fish all night." Just out of sheer obedience, and completely without enthusiasm they head into the deeper water and cast their nets. What the hey!? The nets fill up with so many fish that the nets are about to break. The fishermen call for another boat to come help. Both boat 1 and boat 2 are totally overflowing with fish to the point that they are about to sink. Peter looks at Jesus and falls to his knees. He knows he is in the presence of a Miracle Man. All he can think of is how many mistakes he has made, how bad he has been, and how sinful he feels when he is next to someone so pure.

Jesus said to Andrew and Peter, "Don't be afraid! Guys, come follow Me, and I will make you fishers of men." Andrew and Peter were the first two disciples called by Jesus. James and John, another set of brothers, were in boat 2. They were the next two to be called by Jesus. These four guys remained right inside His innermost circle of friends until Jesus died. After that, they were among the founders of Christianity. They caught many more people than fish, and had the time of their lives reeling them in!

THOUGHTS AND QUESTIONS FOR CONTEMPLATION AND DISCUSSION

Baptism.

- What is the purpose and value of baptism?

- Have you been baptized? If so, did you get baptized by your own choice, or someone else's? If it was by someone else's choice does that count?

- What was John the Baptist's attitude toward Jesus?

- Why and how does he prepare the way for Jesus?

- What are the trees and fruit to which he is referring?

- Why did Jesus get baptized? To model what? For what purpose?

- The Holy Spirit landed on Jesus. What does this mean?

- What do you learn about the Holy Spirit in this text? Who is He? What does He do? (We'll talk about Him a little bit more in future chapters.)

- What was Jesus's three-year assignment?

- What was the assignment of His followers?

- Has the assignment of His followers ever been changed, including the present time?

- As a result of meeting Jesus, what happened to Andrew, and then Peter?

- What is it that compels people who have come to know Jesus to tell others about Him?

People would be walking down the beach and spontaneously be drawn to stay and hang around Jesus, or they would walk 20 miles uphill (literally) just to hear Him speak.

- What must He have been like in person?

- What are some parallels between the double-ton of fish caught in boats 1 and 2, and the assignment of the four fishermen who leave their careers to follow Jesus and fish for men?

- What is the value of obedience to Jesus (in this text specifically)?

- What do you think your reaction would be, and how would you feel, if you were to stand before Jesus? Would it depend on the day, your mood, and what you were in the process of doing when He turned up?

- What do you think may have been the characteristics of these "regular guys" that made Jesus hand select them specifically out of the crowds to come and follow Him?

Note: This text has been influenced by these chapters in the Bible—Mark 1, Luke 5, and John 1.

ENDNOTE

1.   Matthew 16:18.

CLEAN LEPER

A man with leprosy came to him and begged him on his knees, "If you are willing, you can make me clean" (Mark 1:40).

What an exciting time it must have been. Jesus set out with Peter, Andrew, John, and James. They started walking from town to town declaring that the Kingdom of God is at hand. (In my imagination I can hear the soundtrack for this. It has lots of those Jesus songs from the early 1970s like "Spirit in the Sky" by Norman Greenbaum! Good stuff! Please play that at my funeral.) Jesus and the guys would make stops along the way, and crowds would gather to listen to Jesus speak. The people always ended up amazed. The way Jesus shared the Good News was certainly not the way they were used to hearing it in church. Church messages often seemed a bit limp, hypocritical, or boring. Jesus was (and still is) none of these things, that's for sure! Jesus was preaching with authority, and then show-ing the power of God as sick people would come to get prayer for all sorts of healing—physical, emotional, and spiritual. As more and more people were being healed, the gatherings grew larger. Jesus was getting "crowded" out of cities. He ended up finding nature's amphitheaters to speak to the growing throngs.

One day, as Jesus and the disciples were coming down from a mountainside, a man with leprosy came up to them. He knelt down before Jesus. He knew in his heart that if Jesus would only say the word, the leprosy would be healed. This man had been cast out of his town and was living in excommunication in a leper colony. For him to even approach Jesus was culturally inappropriate. In this time and place, if someone were to touch a leper, that person would be classified "unclean," too. There was no cure for leprosy. It was scary and dangerous. This man picked up on something that was different about Jesus. He is approachable. When Jesus looks at people who are in dire straits, He has compassion in His eyes. People feel the love. Plus, everywhere Jesus goes, people are getting healed.

In this particular situation, hope rose up in this leper. With the deepest respect, and a heart full of optimistic desire and desperation, the leper fell to his knees. He said, "Lord, if You are willing, You can set me free from this terrible deterioration. I would no longer be a social outcast. I could go home to my family."

Jesus looked at him and He could see the whole picture—the physical pain, broken heart, wounded spirit, and dilapidated body. He overflowed with love, and He even rested His hand on this "untouchable" man. Jesus didn't need to think twice. He very simply said, "Oh, I AM willing." Instantly the leprosy left. Jesus told the man to go home; he would be welcome back in his hometown now. He was free and well. He would pass all the required medical tests to be allowed back into the community.

Jesus just asked one favor of the healed man. He said not to tell anyone how he had become healthy again. In The Message translation of the Bible, Jesus says, "Your cleansed and obedient life, not your words, will bear witness to what I have done." But the cured leper was so thrilled he ran all over the place telling everyone how he had been healed by Jesus. As a consequence, the crowds around Jesus became even bigger. Everywhere He went, I can imagine that Jesus couldn't even go to the bathroom without people trying to corner Him for a touch from God. (We have a friend, Leif Hetland, with a wonderful healing ministry. He has assured us that this *is* a problem! Oh no! It is a little funny, but think about it, if you are ever at any kind of conference and you run into the speaker in the bathroom—"Be in the know, and let 'em go"! Just a little speaker-friendly etiquette.)

THOUGHTS AND QUESTIONS FOR CONTEMPLATION AND DISCUSSION

- Just for the fun of it, which songs would you like to put in your Jesus soundtrack? Why?

- What was so amazing about Jesus?

- How can His followers help bring a more amazing re-presentation of Him, His character, and His ways?

- How can we avoid being limp, hypocritical, and boring when we are the ones representing Jesus?

- What was it like to be a leper? Name some modern conditions that are similar to leprosy.

- What would it be like to be treated like you are contagious? Have you ever been treated like that for any reason?

- How did Jesus react in the face of something that was considered by the culture to be scary, dangerous, and contagious?

- How can we be more like Him?

Compassionate eyes and a warm touch can be very healing. Inappropriate facial expressions and touch can do damage. How can you know the difference? (I could write chapters on prayer etiquette. With my husband, Brook, in a wheelchair, many people like to pray for him. Boy, we have seen some wild prayer! Some wild in a good way. Some inconsiderate, self-centered, and potentially harmful.)

- What does Jesus see when He looks at a person with problems?

- Jesus said, "I am willing." How can we tap into that willingness that is still available today?

- For extra credit, see Psalm 103:1-6. Which diseases does the Lord heal? You really do want to know the answer to this question! Go there!

- Why did Jesus ask the leper not to tell anyone how he had been healed?

- Why did the man break this one request of Jesus? Is that OK, or not, and why?

- Why would The Message translation of the Bible suggest that Jesus values action over talk? What is the difference?

- How can we be people of our word, not just saying things we don't really mean?

Here is another fun one. If you go to conferences to hear speakers, consider what would be some appropriate and then some inappropriate ways to try to make contact with the speakers. Get goofy, but take it seriously, too.

Note: This text has been influenced by the chapters of: Mark 1, Luke 5, and Matthew 8.

HE HEALED
THEM ALL

At sunset, the people brought to Jesus all who had various kinds of sickness, and laying his hands on each one, he healed them (Luke 4:40).

As Jesus and His followers went from town to town sharing the Good News about the Kingdom of God, there were tons of miraculous healings. The news would spread fast, and big groups of people were gathering.

In one town, four guys carried their paralyzed friend through a huge crowd. Jesus was praying for people inside a building. There would be no way of getting their buddy to the door, let alone through the door. So, these radical believers dug a hole through the roof and lowered the paralyzed man down through the hole. Inspired by the faith of the friends, Jesus healed this paralytic. It is quite possible that the paralyzed guy had run out of faith a long, long time before. Good thing he had friends to carry his body and spirit into the presence of Jesus.

Jesus turned to that paralyzed guy and said, "Your sins are forgiven." This was a controversial moment for the local pastors: (1) everyone knew that only God could pardon sin; (2) Jesus had not been revealed as God; (3) this statement made it clear that He was acting as God, which would be blasphemy if He wasn't actually God. He asked the people, "Which is easier: to say to the paralytic, 'Your sins are forgiven,' or to say, 'Get up, take your mat and walk'?" Since both are impossible to humans, Jesus was making a point. What is impossible for humans is still possible for God. He told the man to pick up his mat and go home. The man stood up, rolled up the mat he had always laid on, and went home free from the burdens of sin and paralysis.

Jesus could do both: Heal people and set them free from the weight of the sin on their conscience. And what is more, Jesus was already in the process of training His followers what they were going to be able to do too, because of their direct relationship with Him. He was given all power and authority by God and then He passed the power and authority to His followers, through the Holy Spirit.

In Luke 7, a Roman centurion sent word to Jesus that his servant was suffering terribly with paralysis. Jesus said, "Take Me to him. Let's go." The centurion knew that it would conflict with Jewish custom for Jesus to enter his home. He also felt unworthy. (I think I can understand that feeling. Standing next to Jesus, I am sure I would be well aware of my shortcomings. Even so, Jesus can convey love and make people feel at ease. I want to be like that, too.) The centurion sent a second message to Jesus saying, "I know that You don't actually have to come to my house to get the job done, just say the word and my servant will be healed."

Jesus was amazed. He hadn't met any of God's people with this level of faith. In all the churches in all the realm, nobody really "got it." It took someone who had never been to church to actually understand the magnitude of Christ's command. (In case you were wondering, I am saying church rather than synagogue to make a point.) Jesus turned to the crowd and said something like, "Do you guys get what is going on here? This centurion isn't one of us, yet he knows the nature of God's authority better than most people in our community!" The centurion's servant was in fact healed at that exact moment. There is another version of this encounter recorded in Matthew 8, told from a different (Matthew's) perspective. It is interesting to me how multiple viewers of the same event will come away from the experience with multiple perspectives. It makes sense really, since we all see things differently, individually.

Next, they headed on to Peter's house. Peter's mother-in-law had a fever; well, that is until Jesus drove the fever out of her. The second the fever left her she got up and started cooking for everyone. Yum! That night many people who were demon possessed were brought to Jesus. He drove out the demons with a word and healed everyone who was sick. Jesus healed them *all*. The Bible says so. He healed diseases, pain, psychosomatic problems, mental illness, and spiritual issues. ALL. As the demons were coming out of people, they recognized Jesus and would try to shout, "You are the Son of God." Of course the demons knew who He was before most people ever really did. Jesus would not allow the demons to speak. He was trying to keep it quiet a little longer that he was the Messiah. He had good reasons for this. Imagine walking down the streets introducing yourself as the Promised One of God! When it was time to leave town, people tried to keep Jesus from going. But He told them, "I must preach the Good News of the Kingdom of God to the other towns also, that is why I was sent."

In pages to come I'll be telling you more fun Bible blurbs about the healing touch of Jesus. Also, there is so much to describe about the miraculous power available to people who allow the Holy Spirit of God to flow through them like a river, or a fiber-optic cable.

This topic is completely relevant and important to us even now, 2,000 years after Jesus died.

─────────────── ∞ ───────────────

THOUGHTS AND QUESTIONS FOR CONTEMPLATION AND DISCUSSION

Miracles and Healings

- What is it about miracles that draw a crowd?

- What is a miracle?

- How often do you think miracles can happen? Are miracles rare? Or could you maybe even experience a miracle today?

- How can one person's faith make a way for someone else to be healed by Jesus?

- Describe the power of the radical faith these friends of the paralytic had. Does a person who is sick need to have faith to get well? That is not a "yes or no" question. Go deeper, looking at both sides.

- What was controversial about the first paralyzed guy getting healed?

- Is it easier for God to forgive sins or to heal someone?

- What are the differences between healing and forgiving? What are the connections?

- What is possible for God? Now might be a good time to memorize a Bible verse. I'd like to suggest Matthew 19:26. Look it up! If you don't have a Bible, google it. This is one of my favorites!

- What was going on with the guys following Jesus, the disciples, during this time? What can we gain from this information?

- Do you know people who feel unworthy of God's love?

- Jesus loved people without considering their nationality, social status, or guilt level. How can you receive this information into your body and soul? How can you convey this to others?

- What can you do to be more like Jesus in this respect?

- Can God heal from a distance or through a friend, a relative, or a colleague's prayers?

- Could God inspire someone to be healed through a message on the TV?

- Could God's love heal someone via the telephone? How so?

- What was special about the faith of the centurion?

- How can some of the things we learn in some churches (and on TV) be damaging to our faith?

- Who did Jesus heal? Why did Jesus heal?

- What things were being healed by Jesus? Is there anything that was not healed?

- Why might demons be more inclined than humans to recognize who Jesus is? Why would Jesus want to keep the demons from talking?

- Do you believe in demons and evil? Why/why not?

- Is there much mention of demons and angels in the Bible? Maybe you will want to look this up online or in a Bible index.

- What are some reasons why Jesus is trying to keep His identity hidden?

- Why was Jesus sent? Who sent Him? Here's a thought: did He send Himself?

Note: This text has been influenced by passages in these chapters in the Bible—Luke 4 and 7; Mark 2; Matthew 9.

PART III

∞

OLD TESTAMENT— FROM THE WILDERNESS TO CONQUEST

THE TEN COMMANDMENTS

Do you remember in the classic movie *The Ten Commandments*[1] when Moses went up on the mountain and came down with the Ten Commandments? Moses had been up there for 40 days and 40 nights with God. God was carving the commandments onto stone tablets with His finger. (In our Bible studies we have joked about God's home video collection and which videos we'd like to watch when we get to Heaven. I'd like to watch this one, and the burning bush part, too! Oh, to see the expression on Moses's face when the bush talked to him!) In the movie *The Ten Commandments,* the stone tablets were portrayed as quite large. The Amplified Bible suggests that these stone tablets "are believed to have been pocket-size, easily carried in one hand."[2] I guess I'll know the truth when I get to Heaven. In my imagination now, though, I see them as approximately 12 inches wide by 18 inches tall, rounded at the top. Yup. It is interesting how much media influences our perceptions about God and the Bible.

OK, on to our story. Moses was coming down the mountain after spending 40 days and 40 nights with Almighty God. Moses could see the people he had just led out of Egypt gathered at the base of the mountain. These folks are the same Israelite "whiners" from the other Moses chapter in Part I. Now they are stuck in the desert. Moses saw that they had made a cow sculpture out of wood and gold, and the people were actually worshiping it! This man-made cow was a model of an Egyptian god. This is a false god—and worshiping anything other than the one True God is called idolatry. One of the plagues in Egypt killed livestock proving that Almighty God is more powerful than cow gods. In fact, each of the plagues in Egypt was sent by the one True God to destroy the Egyptian false gods.

The very first of the Ten Commandments is "Love the Lord God with all your heart and soul and mind and strength." God says, "You shall have no other god before Me." When we value money or time or people or a hobby, or anything else more than God, that is also considered idolatry. Idolatry = worshiping idols. An idol doesn't have to be something that is "bad." It can be anything that is put before God. I think that the United States has made money a god, which is part of the economic problem we're having at this time.

Anyway, Moses got *really* angry seeing the people worshiping the cow idol. Rightly so! But then he threw down the Ten Commandment stone tablets that God had carved. The first draft of the Ten Commandments was shattered on the ground. The earth shook, opened up, and swallowed all of the people who had chosen the cow god. It was a bad day for idol worshipers. Caught in the act. Real God was watching! A while later, Moses would be going up the mountain a second time.

First, God tells him to cut out two blank slabs of stone, and to make a wooden chest. This chest is called an ark. It is made of acacia wood and is for the purpose of holding the stone tablets. The Ark of the Covenant was completely covered in gold, inside and out. It housed God's glory. The word ark is used to label Noah's boat, and again for the box that holds the Ten Commandments. I have also heard of Christians being called arks because we host God's Holy Spirit and God writes His law on our hearts. Later on in history, the enemies of Israel could see the power associated with God's presence being in the Ark of the Covenant. The Philistines captured the box.

(This reminds me of the movie *Raiders of the Lost Ark*.[3] Some interesting Bible humor here, depending on one's interpretation: When the enemies got hold of this box, they developed hemorrhoids. This goes to show that the Presence who is such a blessing to believers doesn't "sit well" with everyone else. No! Ha! That joke stinks, but I love it! Not mine. I borrowed it.[4] It seems that sometimes a little bathroom humor is just enough to keep someone reading! Why? I don't know! For the rest of you, I'm sorry. Please excuse me. Um-hmmm. By the way, many Bible translations say these are "tumors." But hemorrhoids made for a better bad joke, and it is written as "emerods" and "arses" in the Old English Bible translations. So, you choose!)

Now back to more serious stuff. God's presence is certainly not to be "used" or manipulated. It is for high and holy purposes. It is a blessing to God's people and can be quite terrifying to God's enemies, not typically just a pain in the butt.

After making the blank stone slabs and the ark, God instructed Moses to come back up the mountain for the second time. Again Moses stayed there hanging out with God for another 40 days and 40 nights while God wrote a new set of the same commandments. Moses didn't eat food or drink water while he was in God's presence those 40 days. All this is going on during the 40 years that the Israelites spent in the desert. It makes me think that God must be so loving and patient to put up with our shenanigans, over and over and over again. Moses was so precious to God. He had such a good heart. Moses sat up there pleading with God to stay with the Israelites and not turn His back on them even though they were acting like boneheads, numbskulls.

God called these Israelites, the people whom He had delivered from slavery, hardheaded, stiff-necked. He didn't want a whole lot to do with the Israelites at this point after they made an idol out of wood and metal and then worshiped it as a god. Yuck. Yet Moses was negotiating, interceding with God for His mercy. That's how we know it is OK to do that...to intercede for others! We actually have influence with God. He cares what we think. Isn't that cool?! Moses reminded God that these were His people. When Moses came down from the mountain, everyone could see that he had been in God's presence because his face glowed.

In a movie I saw a long, long time ago, there was a joke about the Ten Commandments: Moses is carrying The *Fifteen* Commandments down the mountain and is presenting them to the Israelites. "Here are the fifteen...oop, ahhh, thump, ehhh!" (He stumbles and drops one of the tablets.) "I mean the Ten Commandments."[5] That is silly, and maybe good for a chuckle. I wonder what the other five commandments would have been? Be on time? Keep your word? No littering? Thou shalt recycle? Be flexible? Don't worry; be happy? Do you know what the first ten are? Well? How 'bout looking them up? (The Ten Commandments are listed in Deuteronomy 5 and Exodus 20.)

THOUGHTS AND QUESTIONS FOR CONTEMPLATION AND DISCUSSION

- Which of God's home videos do you want to watch when you get to Heaven?

- How much does Hollywood, and media in general, shape the way you see God and His people?

- How accurately would you say today's media is at capturing God's heart and truth?

- How are Christians generally depicted in TV shows and movies?

- How much of what you watch would you be comfortable watching if God were sitting next to you?

- Think about the wood and gold cow idol. What were the people hoping for?

- What kind of sense does it make to worship something man-made like this?

- What things do you make a little too important, that is to say more important than God? Kids? Job? Money? Shoes? Food? The daily news? Cookies?

- God is watching. Does that influence the way you think, speak, behave?

- Should the idea that God is watching influence you a little bit more?

- With that in mind, what in your life do you purpose to change?

- What is God's presence?

- How could the presence of God be a blessing to His people, but terrifying to His enemies?

- Why would this be true of a "loving" God?

- How should God's presence be treated?

Describe how loving and patient God must be. He doesn't like our yuck, but He loves us through it. When all is said and done, He forgives a whole lot of stuff. Make a list. How should we treat His mercy and grace?

Regarding intercession, Moses pleaded with God to stay with His people. How would you go about doing that for a loved one who is following idols or false gods?

When Moses had spent time in God's presence, it was obvious to others. He glowed.

- How can you apply that to your life?

- What about your appearance might look different and more appealing if you got a "faith lift"?

- Now for the biggie: What are the Ten Commandments? Check the references and look them up (Deuteronomy 5 and Exodus 20)! Put them in your own words. How are you doing with following the Ten Commandments?

Note: This text has been influenced by sections of these chapters in the Bible—Exodus 19–20, 24–25, 32, 34 Deuteronomy 9-10, 34.

ENDNOTES

1. *The Ten Commandments,* Cecil B. DeMille, Paramount, 1956.

2. Amplified Bible, footnotes for Exodus 34:4; Zondervan, 1987.

3. *Indiana Jones and the Raiders of the Lost Ark*, Steven Spielberg and George Lucas, Paramount, 1981.

4. Bill Johnson, Bethel Church Message, "Feeding Alligators"; www.ibethel.tv, 3/15/2009.

5. *History of the World, Part 1,* Mel Brooks, 20th Century Fox, 1981. This is not a Christian film, and some content may be questionable for some people. Also, the filmmakers took a lot of creative license.

JOSHUA

Way back in the first story of Moses, we left Moses and the Israelites in the desert waiting for the last guy under the "40 year" desert detainment to die. It looks like that guy was Moses. It is fitting to note that Moses aged very well. At 120 years old, he was strong and his eyesight was still great, then it was just time for him to go home to God. This is biblical proof that people don't have to fall apart as they age! The real Fountain of Youth is God! Since Moses was at the end of his life, it was time to install the new leader. Moses put his hands on Joshua and prayed to transfer the wisdom God had given him onto Joshua, who would now be the leader of the Israelites.

Way back when Joshua was 40, he had gone on a 40-day scouting adventure into the Promised Land. Joshua and Caleb had known that they could "take" the Promised Land. They knew God was with them. The rest of the scouts got overwhelmed and felt as small as grasshoppers compared to the enemy nation who had looked like giants to them. The fear in those ten scouts poisoned the whole camp. Joshua and Caleb were outnumbered. Because these ten other guys chickened out, the whole nation had to wander for 40 years.

Now that the first generation was deceased, the restraint was lifted. It was time to head into the Promised Land. At this point, God has a long talk with Joshua, informing him: "Everywhere you put your feet will become your land." God goes on to say, "Read your Bible, pray, be courageous, and don't get discouraged. That is the way to success and prosperity."

Now I need to tell you, one of my favorite Bible stories is right here in the middle of this Joshua story. Joshua sent two spies into Jericho. They ended up staying with Rahab, a prostitute. The king of Jericho found out they were there, but Rahab hid them. She told the two spies that the whole country was melting in fear of the Israelites. They had heard (1) of how powerful and awesome God is, (2) of the miracles from those days back in Egypt, and (3) of all of the signs and wonders that went with the Israelites because God was with them. As a result, Jericho had been dreading the day when the Israelites would come to battle them. They had been in fear of that day for 40 years now.

Rahab helped the spies escape in exchange for their protection when the Israelites would come back to conquer Jericho. I'll tell you ahead of time, they did protect her, and her whole family, too. She got to know God. She married an honorable man. And…she is recorded as a great-great-great-ancestor of Jesus, Himself. Not everyone knows that Jesus has a woman restored from prostitution in His lineage. You see, God didn't see her as a prostitute, but as a forebearer of the King of kings. God sees people from the perspective of how He created us, our destiny—not our past. Man, talk about second chances and divine grace! I love that story.

Joshua gets the army ready to attack. He tells them to get into "holy mode" because God is going to do some amazing things. They grab the Ark of the Covenant, which you may know from *Indiana Jones* and *The Ten Commandments*. They head toward the Jordan River. When they step into the river with the Ark of the Covenant, the water stops flowing, and they walk across on dry land (like Moses at the Red Sea). When the Israelites had crossed the Red Sea they were saved, now they are walking into the Promised Land. (Many Christians settle for being saved and never advance into the Promised Land. Hey guys, the Kingdom of God is at hand, at hand, at hand! Grab it!)

On the other side of the Jordan, the Israelites stop in their tracks to build a monument of national unity in honor of this miracle. The monument is made from rocks that had been in the middle of the river. Then they're back on their way to conquer seven nations. There were 40,000 armed Israelites heading for Jericho. The enemy nations heard about the Jordan drying and they were totally terrified. (What a great strategy for battle: Arrange a miracle before you arrive! It really freaks out the opposition.)

As Joshua was approaching Jericho, he came upon a man with a drawn sword. Joshua asked the man if he was "for them" or "against them." "Neither," he replied, "but as commander of the army of the Lord I have now come." Joshua realized that he was standing in front of an angel, or maybe even God appearing in human form! He knew this was a holy moment. He asked what message the Lord had for him. This commander of the Lord's army replied, "Take off your sandals, for the place where you are standing is holy." Joshua did so, honoring the holy moment. (The "Burning Bush" had said the same thing to Moses before Moses had gone to release Israel from slavery in Egypt.)

At this point the Lord has another powwow with Joshua. Catch this, it is important. God says, "I have already given Jericho into your hands, now go and march around the city walls." The victory is guaranteed in advance. It is already a done deal. Now, look at this crazy military maneuver. Joshua instructs seven priests sounding trumpets and more priests carrying the Ark of the Covenant to march around the city walls along with the armed guard and the rear guard. They went around the city one time, no chit-chat allowed. They did this one time per day for six consecutive days. On the seventh day they did the same thing, except on the seventh day they went around the city walls seven times. The seventh time around they shouted a loud victory cry and the city walls tumbled to the ground. Then the Israelites rushed into the city and took the land God had promised them so very long ago. This is how God's people win battles in the Promised Land.

THOUGHTS AND QUESTIONS FOR CONTEMPLATION AND DISCUSSION

Moses had an exceptional relationship with God, and he aged really well.

- How much of a correlation do you feel there is between being God-centered and healthy?

- How could knowing God improve a person's health? Why?

- How did Moses transfer wisdom to Joshua? How does this work?

- What was the difference in the perspective of Joshua and Caleb versus the rest of the scouts?

- What was the dominant mindset?

- How could fear dominate the decision- making process when God had shown up so powerfully?

- How does this happen in your life? How often?

- What is the recipe God gives Joshua for success and prosperity? Which of these ingredients are missing from your life? What are you doing well?

- What do you think of the news that Rahab gave the spies?

- What had been going on in Jericho for the 40 years while the Israelites were being held in the desert?

- How can this change your perspective on some of the difficulties in your life?

- Why would God select Rahab to be an ancestor of Jesus?

- Have you met anyone who has significantly turned his or her life around with the help of God? How did it happen?

- What are signs and wonders? How are they like road signs showing us the way to God, all the while making us wonder about how great God is and how much we can accomplish when He is with us?

The river was a barrier on the way to the Promised Land.

- How hard was it for God's people to get to the other side of this barrier?

- How can you apply this to your own life?

- How did they honor this moment?

- How should you honor God in times of amazing breakthrough?

- What are some of the interesting things that happen with the commander of the Lord's army?

- What does this experience have in common with the Burning Bush experience?

- Why was the ground holy?

- Which side was the commander on?

- How often do you suspect that God does *not* pick sides when people are in a conflict?

- Does God have a favorite football team?

Contemplate the expressions, "I have already" and "now go" as they are used by God. Some victories are guaranteed in advance. All we have to do is follow through with our part.

- Can you perceive any overwhelming future victories waiting for your participation with God?

- How do God's people win battles in the Promised Land? It took following instructions and daily obedience. What else?

- Now, what is your next step?

Note: This text has been influenced by these passages in the Bible—Joshua 1–6; Deuteronomy 34:5-9.

DEBORAH AND BARAK

The Bible literally reports that "once again" Israel did evil in God's eyes. As a consequence, God has let Israel fall into the hands of Canaan—the land that Joshua had conquered, not so very long ago. Well, now there is this really mean guy with 900 iron chariots, state-of-the-art warfare equipment of the day, oppressing Israel. His name is Sisera, but you wouldn't really wanna nickname him "Sissy." He'd probably just kill you. He is the commander of the Canaanite army. A terror. This guy is so cruel that people are almost afraid to even go outside. A lot of village life is at a standstill. Maybe no lingering happy hour at the well, few parties. Hiking and shopping are done in haste, when necessary. People even seemed to avoid Main Street, as it were. Travel is reduced to back roads and alleyways. Taxation and military oppression are putting a major damper on all aspects of life, and the Israelites are once again calling out to God for help.

At this time Deborah is the local leader. Imagine that, a woman leader in the Old Testament. She is judge over Israel and she hears all the civil disputes in the country. In her position of great influence, she calls the military leader of Israel, Barak. She tells him that the

Lord has called him to organize 10,000 men to go battle Sisera. Barak responds that he would be willing to do this, but only if she will go with him. She says she will, but then he must understand that Sisera would then be defeated at the hand of a woman.

Gotta love Barak, he isn't threatened by this at all. He seems to feel that triumph will be assured because of Deborah's joint effort with him. I am impressed with his ability to share victory with this valiant female. This is a characteristic I particularly admire in men. My darling husband is like that. He is in no way diminished when I am the one with the good idea. He weighs my suggestions and often helps me refine a plan of action. Then we advance as a team, more than twice as strong as we would be as individuals. But wait! That is just my interpretation. There is another possibility here. (Isn't it interesting that there can be more than one interpretation in a Bible story!) Maybe Barak needed Deborah for another reason. It is possible that he simply didn't have faith for this victory, but he knew that she did. She was a prophet of God. She had the inside track on the prophesied outcome. But Barak? He wasn't as sure. He may have been scared, even a coward. Or? Maybe Barak understood the power that strong faith in God can have to influence the air around us, and the spiritual realm. Any way you slice it, Barak needed to tap into Deborah's close connection with God. So he did.

Back to the story: Barak and Deborah round up 10,000 men. The Lord Himself influences the route that the enemies choose. The Israelites were then able to corner all of the 900 chariots, and the whole enemy army. It is truly against all odds. Without God's sword (God's involvement) it would have been impossible. The Israelites are outnumbered and have inferior equipment. Yet Sisera's charioteers and all his warriors are forced to flee on foot. The Israelites conquer them.

Sisera also escapes on foot. Uh-oh, who's the "Sissy" now that all of his big, scary iron chariots are stuck between a rock and a hard place? He ends up hiding in the tent of a woman named Jael. Jael's husband seems to have been buddying up with the bad guys, perhaps a traitor, or maybe just playing it safe. When Sisera sees this fair female (Jael) smiling and waving to him, he feels safe in her care. I picture Jael as a housewife, except she lives in a tent. She's a tent wife, and she's tough. She built the tent herself, with a workman's hammer and heavy-duty spikes. That is just part of her housewife routine. If there are any women out there who are looking for strong female role models in the Bible, I recommend they check out Jael in Judges 4 and 5. She has quite a special technique for overthrowing the biggest bad guy of the day!

First she makes evil Commander Sisera feel secure and comfortable. She tells him, "Don't be afraid. I'll keep you hidden. Now get some rest." Then she gives him a nice glass of milk in fine china, and covers him up ever so gently. But then when he drifts off to sleep, she drives a tent stake through his head and nails him to the ground, dead. When Barak came by, she went out to meet him saying, "Sir, I have something here I think you ought to see. I've got the guy you're looking for!" This whole scenario turns out to be very encouraging to the nation of Israel. They were then able to overcome the Canaanite rule. They grew stronger and stronger until they destroyed the Canaanite king as well.

After all this, Deborah and Barak sang a great song of worship to the Lord. In this song, it is mentioned that even the river and the stars were on Deborah's side and had joined in the battle. They instructed rulers and kings to take note of the greatness of God. Deborah arose as a great leader and wise mother to the nation of Israel. Under the oppression of Canaan, people had been unhappy, living dull lives of defeat and depression. Deborah stood strong, with God as her Advisor, and arranged a strategy to defeat a cruel conqueror. The land relaxed and came back to life under her great leadership. There was peace for 40 years.

THOUGHTS AND QUESTIONS FOR CONTEMPLATION AND DISCUSSION

God had led Joshua into the Promised Land. Two hundred years have passed. Now Israel is being oppressed again.

- What the heck happened to Israel?

- After a history of great miracles and deliverance, how do the Israelites end up back in bondage?

- How does anyone ever end up in bondage?

- Have you ever been terrorized by someone to the extent that you are afraid to leave your house, but you're afraid to be in your house, too?

- What about being terrorized by the fear of falling back into a problem lifestyle? Or, have you ever just had a general feeling of anxiety, for no good reason?

- How can you/people start to break free from fear?

- Could the honor and the victory have belonged to Barak?

- Why do you think Barak insisted that Deborah go with him?

- Was this decision a sign of security, insecurity, fear, faith, or something else?

- Where was Barak putting his trust?

- What is the Bible's position on using women to secure a military victory?

- What is the Bible's position on women in positions of judicial and political influence?

- How can strong women support men who are discouraged, without detracting from their value and skills?

- What is the sword of the Lord?

- How does God influence the route that the enemies choose?

- What would the Israelites have to have done *not* to win this battle?

- How often do you think God makes a way for something to happen that seems to be impossible?

- What happens if you don't do your part, and therefore that miraculous victory can never take place?

- I wonder what it will feel like when I try to explain my perspective on so many missed opportunities as I stand before God and He weighs my life. Imagine yourself in that situation.

Talk about a housewife's ability to use her daily tasks and natural gifting to defeat a powerful enemy—Jael saved the nation!

- What resources did Jael tap into to overthrow the source of oppression? Discuss how much influence a wife and mother can have, if she sets herself to it.

- If a husband is following an enemy force, does a wife have to carry that label?

- How can a wife stay loyal to her husband and still over-throw the opposing forces?

- Maybe you are in a relationship with someone who is being loyal to something harmful. Is it possible to love someone but not support their lifestyle? Or, does the word "codependent" come to mind? What kind of role model is Jael?

- Into the hands of which woman was Sisera delivered? Defend your choice.

- Why did Deborah and Barak turn this big event into a song?

- Do you find it easier to memorize sentences when they are set to music?

- Have you ever noticed the power of music to influence your mood?

- What was the nature of Deborah and Barak's song?

- Why do you think God created music?

- What does it mean to sing to God?

Note: This text has been influenced by the chapters of Judges 4 and 5 in the Bible.

SAMSON

This Samson story is bizarre and complex. You should read it for yourself. It is found in Judges 13 through 16. By the way, I have recently found that reading from a translation of the Bible called *The Message* makes the Bible more understandable. You probably noticed that I have referred to this translation a few times already in this book. It is written in regular ol' vernacular American English, rather than scholarly language, or Shakespearean English. It sort of sounds like the way you might talk when you're out to lunch with some buddies. I have found that when I want to just sit and read the Bible in a relaxed way (like at bedtime), *The Message* is the translation I pick up. Make some time to check it out. You can even read the Bible online or on a smart phone (sources to follow)!

Some background to the Samson history: The Israelites have been in the Promised Land for over 200 years. It is recorded that the Israelites' attitudes and behaviors have gone wrong…yet again. At this point, God has lifted His protection over Israel. Now the bad guys, the Philistines this time, have taken control of the country. The "40" comes as Samson is born and raised. He will be the one to launch the deliverance of Israel from the Philistines, after the Philistines have ruled over Israel for 40 years.

The story begins: There is a lady who cannot have children. The Angel of the Lord comes to her and declares she will have a son. She does. The parents name him Samson, and they ask God to teach them how to raise him. Samson is to never to drink alcohol and never to cut his hair. He will also be kept ritually clean from the time of his birth. So far, so good.

Samson had a weakness. Many will say that it is when his hair is cut he loses his strength, and that is true. I, however, would say his real weakness is foreign girls. He just can't resist these women, and if they're dangerous he seems to want them even more. Three times he makes himself vulnerable because of bad choices in women. The last time it costs his vision and ultimately his life.

In the meantime, Samson is on his way to visit his parents when a lion starts to attack him. The Spirit of the Lord comes on Samson and he gets exceedingly strong. He rips the lion apart with his bare hands. Next time he's in the area, he visits the lion's carcass. It was full of honey, which he brought as a gift to his parents. But he never told them about the lion. I don't know what this means, but it seems God is in the lion mystery. Later, Samson turns this lion incident into a riddle to make a bet with 30 guys. The only problem is, Samson has a bad-girl bride who knows the answer to the riddle. She leaks it to the 30 guys, a group of enemy Philistines. They were threatening her family. She turned on the tears and got Samson to give her the answer to the riddle. Why, I just don't know. She could have told him she was being threatened, but instead she manipulated him.

Having lost the bet, Samson beats up and strips naked those 30 guys who had cheated him. He also ends up giving this wife away. The story gets confusing because Samson goes to visit her after he gives her back. Why? Maybe he thinks she's still his wife? Maybe he can't let go? I don't know. Her father won't let him go near her. Samson gets irate and burns down the whole village by tying torches to 300 foxes. (Huh? Like where do you even get 300 foxes on short notice?) He's totally out for revenge and is hating the Philistines. He seems to believe he has a right to go wrecking stuff. Looks to me like Sammy has a temper!

The Philistines decide to take Samson prisoner. It comes to pass that Samson is tied up by some of his own countrymen to be handed over to them. Of course Samson has supernatural strength, so the ropes seem to just disintegrate as he moves his arms. Samson decides to strike back. Now see if you can catch this quirky little Bible joke:

> And Samson said, "With the jawbone of an ass, heaps upon heaps, with the jaw of an ass have I slain a thousand men" (Judges 15:16 KJV).

OK, it wasn't clear to me either. I personally find the King James translation of the Bible difficult to understand. But, I have to thank the King James translation for referring to this weapon as "the jaw-bone of an ass." The New International Version says, "With a donkey's jawbone I have made donkeys of them." Combining the two trans-lations I have found that Samson makes an "ass" out of 1,000 people by beating them to death with the jawbone of a donkey. They were mocking him, but Samson wins. I guess you could say that Samson whomped them with an "ass bone." An interesting twist which proba-bly reads best in the original language. Next thing you know, Samson leads the country as Judge of Israel for 20 years.

Flash forward in time: Samson is with a prostitute. His enemies lock him inside the city gates so they can capture him. City gates are huge and strong, but Samson just rips the doors off the hinges and carries them down the road a bit, and he gets away.

Now for one of the most memorable Samson stories—his well-known relationship with Delilah, the classic Bible bad girl. She's working for the Philistines for a payoff in silver. She's trying to get the secret of Samson's strength so he can be captured. He gives her a false clue as to how to steal his strength. Delilah ties him up in the way he described he could be overpowered. Bad guys are hiding in the closet, ready to take Samson away. But, of course, Samson breaks free. Unbelievably, this happens three times. She tried to trap him once; she tried to trap him twice; she tried to trap him three times. Why oh why oh why did he tell her his big secret after that? Even God's strongest warriors are not invulnerable to the charms of a woman. In this case, it is a wicked and manipulative woman. "Don't cha love me Sammy-whammy? Don't cha trust me snuggly Sam?" She piled on the charm and learned how to destroy him. He caved in and told her about his hair being his source of strength.

While Samson was sleeping with his head on Delilah's lap, the Philistines shaved his hair. That did the trick. He lost his strength. He woke up figuring he would just shake free like he had always done before. I wonder if he had been thinking he would always be safe in the hands of danger because God had let him get away so many times before? Well, not this time. He pushed it too far. God's strength was gone from him. He had traded his God-given gift to play cat and mouse with a temptress. The Philistines put him in chains and threw him in prison. Oh, and then they gouged his eyes out, too.

But wait! There's more! While he was in prison his hair started to grow back. And you can probably guess what that means.

The rulers of the Philistines decided to make a mockery of Samson. They were having a celebration where all the top leaders and officials were gathered together to offer sacrifices to their false god, dagon. There were 3,000 of the most important Philistines meeting inside a huge temple. Blind Samson is brought forth to entertain them. He prays to God, asking for a last moment of strength, and his last request is granted. He knocks down the most critical weight-bearing pillars in this huge temple. The entire building collapses and kills everyone, Samson included. He killed more Philistines when he died than when he lived.

It is never too late to do the right thing! In eternity and in Heaven's Hall of Faith, Samson is on record as a man who "through faith conquered kingdoms, administered justice, and gained what was promised...whose weakness was turned to strength..." (Hebrews 11:33-34).

THOUGHTS AND QUESTIONS FOR CONTEMPLATION AND DISCUSSION

I mostly use these five translations on a regular basis for studying the Bible: New International Version, New American Standard Bible, Amplified, New King James, and *The Message*. Explore some different translations. Compare what they say, and how they say it.

- Do you read the Bible? Have you ever tried?
- Have you ever heard of *The Message* Bible version?
- If you do read the Bible, what percentage of what you're reading do you understand?
- Why would God lift His protection when the Israelites' attitudes and behaviors had gone wrong, leaving room for bad guys to come take over Israel?
- How does God provide another chance for His people to get out of the mess they are in?
- Has God sent someone into your life to help you get a breakthrough?
- Has He sent you to someone else?

Samson was a strong man who had a weakness.

- How well did Samson manage his weakness?
- What are some areas in your life that you would identify as risks of weakness?

- Develop some strategies for preventing yourself from getting into the wrong places, and with the wrong people.

Using Samson's wife as a model of what *not* to do, pay attention to your behavior patterns, and those used by significant people in your life.

- Do you have any backward strategies for accomplishing things, like emotional bribery, nagging, manipulation, crying and whining? Identify them and consider how you can change negative behavior patterns in your environment.

Samson justified doing something that is wrong because of the other people's wrong behavior.

- Is revenge and retaliation a responsible reaction?

- What might be a better technique for solving problems?

- How can forgiveness or non-retaliation break some revenge cycles?

- If you could have a supernatural power, which one would you like? I think it would be cool to fly or teleport! (Teleporting would be faster, but flying seems more fun. Oh, I'd also like some form of super-vision. Or maybe....) How about you?

- Does Samson make good use of his supernatural strength?

- How much of the time did Samson spend using his supernatural strength to clean up messes which he had made?

- Seriously, what is the deal with Samson's attraction to Delilah? Does he not see any danger there?

- Why did he stay with her?

- How can you spot deceit and manipulation before your heart gets hooked on a bad person?

- What is the best thing to do with the gifting that God has put in you? Is this to be taken lightly, or taken for granted?

- When you use your gifting for selfish purposes, who misses out?

- Is there a situation in your life you secretly believe you can keep getting away with? Do you have a completely clean conscience reading this question? Often there are warnings before consequences. It is usually a smart exercise to inventory your conscience to make sure nothing other than God has a hold on your body, heart, mind, or soul.

- Did Samson end well?

- Could he have done better with what God had given him?

- What can you learn from Samson's life that you can apply to your own life?

Notes: This text has been influenced by the chapters of Judges 13 through 16.

The following online Bible website offers a variety of Bible versions including *The Message*: www.biblegateway.com. My husband uses a phone app and computer system called accordance, www.accordancebible.com.

PART IV

NEW TESTAMENT— ON THE WAY TO THE CROSS

LOAVES AND FISH

So they sat down in groups of hundreds and fifties. Taking the five loaves and the two fish and looking up to heaven, he gave thanks and broke the loaves. Then he gave them to his disciples to distribute to the people. He also divided the two fish among them all (Mark 6:40-41).

The apostles had just come back from a special outing, a genuine field trip! Jesus had given them the authority and assignment to go out and "do" the things they had been learning from Him. Now they were back, and they couldn't wait to tell Jesus about all the amazing things they had done and seen. Of course there was always that huge crowd surrounding Jesus nowadays. Jesus is excited to see His gang and wants to hear their stories, so they get into a boat and head out for a quiet place. One problem—the people on the shore see where the boat is headed, and the crowd runs along the shoreline gathering even more people along the way.

When Jesus and the apostles drop anchor in the quiet place, there is an even bigger crowd than the one they have left! Gah! Now they are in a remote place where there isn't even a McDonald's or Taco Bell. The cool thing about Jesus is that He sees how hungry these people are. They are not so much hungry for the type of food that will fill their bellies. Rather, they hunger for the type of food that will sustain their souls throughout their lives—the words of Jesus are food to our spirits. These folks totally want to hear what He has to say, even if it means they have to go without burgers for days. So, Jesus begins teaching them cool stuff about God.

Long after lunch time, the disciples come to Jesus and point out that people are going to need to eat and there isn't even a pizzeria nearby. (Now don't forget that these guys still want to have their "alone-time" with Jesus.) They suggest that Jesus should send the crowds away to go get food. Jesus tells the disciples, "You feed them." Huh? They respond that it would take eight months of wages to feed a crowd this big. Jesus asks them to inventory all the food on-site. There were five loaves of bread and two fish.

Jesus told His guys to get the crowd organized. The people broke into groups of 50 to 100 people. Jesus took the bread and fish and prayed. He thanked God and then broke the bread into smaller chunks, and the fish, too. Jesus handed the bread and fish to His disciples and told them to distribute food to all the people. As the disciples handed out the bread and fish, the food never ran out. Imagine that! All the people ate and were satisfied. There were 5,000 men, plus women and children. That means there could have been as many as 10,000 people, maybe more. After everyone was finished eating, the disciples cleaned up the area, gathering twelve baskets of leftovers. God had worked with Jesus's disciples. He had partnered with them to show them that if they had enough faith in Him, and if they would respond out of obedience instead of unbelief, they could do a miracle with God's help. If they learned the lesson Jesus was trying to teach them, then they could feed the masses.

These guys might not have really learned it the first time through. They did this miracle more than once. Repeat the lesson. The next time Jesus was in another remote place with 4,000 men, plus women and children. The story goes like this: They were having a miracle party. Deaf, mute, blind, disabled…all sorts of people with all sorts of problems were brought to Jesus and set in front of Him. He healed them, and then it turned into a praise party. Everyone was praising God. He is such a good God! As the party was coming to an end, Jesus realizes that they hadn't eaten for three days. He had compassion on the people. He wanted to feed the crowd so they wouldn't collapse on their way home.

Again, He had the disciples find out what food was available. In other words, what do they already have to work with, to start with? He wasn't making something from nothing; they were multiplying what was already in front of them. It turns out there were seven loaves and some fish. Jesus did the same thing as the last time. He gave thanks to God for what they had and started to break the bread into chunks. He had the disciples hand out the bread and fish. It is important to note that Jesus gave thanks and blessed the food, but the food was multiplied in the disciples' hands. They were very much part of this miracle. Dude, I totally want to do disciple stuff! I'm a disciple, why not me!? I am going to press into God for more miraculous breakthrough!

Here are a few other fun things to note:

1) "Increase" or "multiplication" always started with an attitude of gratitude for what they already had.

2) They handed out the food freely, as if they were sure there would be enough.

3) When they started with less, they fed more people and had more leftovers.

4) There were always more leftovers than the raw material they started with.

5) They always collected and ate the leftovers.

That is good stewardship!

Let's review:

Give thanks to God.

Start with what you have.

Give it away freely.

Don't be wasteful.

———— ∞ ————

THOUGHTS AND QUESTIONS FOR CONTEMPLATION AND DISCUSSION

- What does it mean "to be hungry for spiritual things"?

- How can feeding the soul sustain the body?

- What could God teach that would be so fulfilling that people wouldn't be consumed with thoughts about food (thoughts about chocolate!)?

- How often do you take a good, close look at your own motives when you are doing things for God or for others?

- Why is it beneficial to appraise the motives of our hearts?

- Is it possible to do good things for bad reasons?

- How can you balance taking care of your own needs, and serving others? Generally speaking, it is wonderful to help out and serve others. Some people do too much and end up exhausted. Many other people are sitting on the sidelines assuming somebody else is going to get things done.

- When you see someone in need of help, or something that needs to be done, what is your response?

- Who performed the miraculous feedings of the multitudes?

- In whose hands did the food multiply?

- How can you apply ⸳ ⸳ Bible verses to your own life circumstances?

- Did the discipl ⸳ays J ⸳ the lessons the first time through? Repetition is ⸳ ⸳ to learn things.

- What is the biblical at ⸳ ⸳ eating leftovers?

- Take another look a ⸳ ⸳ ⸳at is it?

- How does godly co ⸳ ⸳ in this text?

- How many of thes ⸳ ⸳ d ⸳licate in this day and age?

- How do miracles hap ⸳ and who makes them happen?

- What godly attitudes and behaviors accompany miracles like this?

- What do *you* have to work with at the moment?

- How could you do more with what you have, if God were to give you a jump-start?

- How could you end up with more "leftovers" than the raw material you started with? Imagine scenarios, dream with God.

- Are there any cool thoughts or dreams blooming in your soul when you start to contemplate this text?

Reading Recommendations: I have recently heard of several times when food multiplication has taken place, in "real life." I'll recommend two authors so you can read how this and other mind-boggling miraculous stuff is going on right now! Warning: These books have been known to raise faith in a radically cool way!

- *Compelled by Love: How to Change the World through the Simple Power of Love in Action* by Heidi Baker (Charisma House, 2008).

- *Always Enough: God's Miraculous Provision among the Poorest Children on Earth* by Heidi Baker (Chosen Books, 2003).

- *The Supernatural Power of a Transformed Mind: Access to a Life of Miracles* by Bill ███████ (Destiny Image Publishers, 2005).

- *Face to Face with God* by Bill Johnson (Charisma House, 2007).

Note: This text has been influenced by the chapters of Matthew 14 and 15, and Mark 6 and 8.

CALM THE STORM

He said to his disciples, "Why are you so afraid? Do you still have no faith?" (Mark 4:40).

I t should almost go without saying that with so many fishermen on the team, Jesus and the disciples would travel by sea a good bit. There was a fleet of boats; I don't know how many. One evening, at the end of the day, Jesus suggested to this group of experienced seamen that they cross the sea by night. They all jumped into their boats and headed out to deep water. Jesus took this opportunity to get some rest and was rocked to sleep by the waves. About halfway across, a huge storm hit. They were being tossed around as if they were in toy boats. Water was coming over the sides. Even these big, burly, rough and tough, experienced fishermen were terrified. It must have been an incredible squall. The disciples woke up Jesus and said to Him, "Don't You care if we drown!?" (Which really is a funny thing to say to the Guy who came to save the world.[1])

You may pause to wonder how Jesus could be sleeping while "all hell" is breaking loose around Him. Keep in mind that Jesus's soul is anchored in Heaven. I wonder what these seamen really thought He could do about the problem. Did they just want to invite Him into their terror? Did they hope He (the Miracle Man) could do something about a storm at sea? Well, Jesus is the answer to the storm (then and now). Quite simply, He stands up and literally speaks to the storm, "Quiet! Be still." Immediately the wind and waves go calm. Problem solved. He turns to the disciples and asks them why they were afraid. "Have you no faith?" He asks. I'm not sure which was more terrifying—being in the storm, or standing next to the One who can command the wind and the waves.

In any case, if you are in a storm, you need God with you. That is one good reason to learn more about Jesus. I don't just mean physical storms, but emotional and spiritual storms, too. If the Spirit of Jesus lives in you, you can rest while the world is raging all around you. If you know Him even better, you can sometimes even command the storm to stop.[2]

Another time Jesus sent the disciples out to sea while He stayed behind to pray. He told them He would catch up with them later. Earlier that day He had heard that His buddy John the Baptist had been beheaded. He needed to hang out with God, to mourn for John, and to get His strength back. So the disciples sailed off without Him. While Jesus sat high on a mountain praying, He somehow became aware that a storm was hitting the guys at sea, and their boats were being flung about and threatened by the wind and waves.

My recently retrained thinking on this topic is that, having learned by experience, the disciples should have at least *tried* to tell the wind to be still. But it didn't go down like that. Although Jesus had trained them for such a situation as this, He was going to have to rescue them again. Jesus walked out to them, walking on the water. Now the disciples weren't expecting *that!* They were freaked out thinking they were seeing a g-g-g-g-ghost. Jesus told them it was Him, and not to be afraid. Peter caught something that none of the other disciples got. He said, "If it is You, tell me to come to You walking on the water, too." You see, Peter recognized the power in the words of Christ. When God speaks, there is the ability for the impossible to become possible.

Jesus said, "OK, go for it, Peter. Come." Peter got out of the boat and started walking on the water toward Jesus. But then he felt the wind of the storm, and fear gripped him. As soon as he doubted, he sank into the sea. The way I see this scene, Jesus let out a big laugh of love. He was so proud of Peter. I can imagine the other guys making fun of Peter for sinking. But none of them actually got to walk on water, only Peter did! I imagine that Jesus said to Peter, "Dude, what happened?! You were actually walking on water! Why did you start to doubt at that point?"

It's about keeping our focus on Jesus, not the wind and the waves. Remember this: Peter walked on water! When Peter and Jesus both got into the boat, the wind and waves calmed down. Everyone on the boat went nuts in praise. It was becoming much clearer to them who this Jesus really is. When they got to the other side of the sea, people recognized Jesus. Word spread all over that Jesus had arrived. His reputation had preceded Him. Sick people came from all around. People would try to get close enough to Jesus to touch His clothing. Yet again, all who touched Him were healed.

THOUGHTS AND QUESTIONS FOR CONTEMPLATION AND DISCUSSION

Imagine how bad that storm must have been to make those tough-guy, experienced seamen wake Jesus in a panic.

- Why do you think they woke Him up to ask Him if He cared?

- Do you ever wonder if God is sleeping while you are in a crisis?

- What does it mean that Jesus could sleep in the storm because His soul was anchored in Heaven? Can you do that, too? If so, how do you get started, or at least go to the next level?

- What was the storm?

- How could Jesus command it to stop?

- What does faith have to do with not being afraid during storms?

- What are other options?

- What kinds of storms are there? Hint: Storms in life are not always weather related.

- How can you learn to rest in the storm?

Jesus mourned for John the Baptist; Jesus escaped to pray often.

- Does God mourn for people who die? When and when not? Why and why not?

- Why did Jesus pray?

- What things did He talk to God about, and why?

- If Jesus is God, why was He always talking to God?

Jesus was many miles away while the disciples were caught in a thick storm.

- How could He see what was going on?

- Was it physical vision, or spiritual vision?

- Mark 6 indicates that Jesus had planned to see how they were doing and pass by. I'm thinking the disciples should have handled the situation differently. Any ideas how? How can you apply this lesson to your own life?

- What do you think about Jesus walking on water?

- What would be special about walking on water?

- How do you view what happened to Peter? Why did he sink? Is this something to laugh at?

- Do you "get out of the boat"?

- When you encounter others who are trying to do the impossible with the help of Jesus, what is your reaction to them? Admiration? Mockery? Confusion? Emulation?

- Have you been getting new revelations lately about who Jesus is? Like what?

- How about new revelations about who you are or who you could be because of Jesus?

His touch of healing.

- Does it really say that *"all"* who touched Him were healed in the end of Matthew 14?

- What part of this can we tap into today with the same Holy Spirit Who raised Jesus from the dead living in His believers? (See Romans 8:11)?

Note: This text has been influenced influenced by the chapters of Mark 4 and 6; Matthew 14.

ENDNOTES

1. Several references in this chapter have been adapted from Bill Johnson's teachings: www.ibethel.tv.

2. John 14:11-12.

PHARISEES

PART 1

This may be a stretch for a 40 story, but I wanted to introduce you to the Pharisees. The Pharisees were a Jewish sect from around the time that Jesus was living (approximate dates: 100 BC–AD 100).[1] The Pharisees were some of the best-educated religion scholars of the day. They are best known for their especially strict adherence to the laws Moses recorded in the Old Testament. They also made up a bunch of extra rules, and piled them on top of God's set of laws which was already complete. In their interpretation and enforcement of all of these rules and laws, they made it difficult for regular folks to live realistic lives.

I'll try to make up an adequate example: There is a law in the Ten Commandments that says "keep the Sabbath holy." Our common culture translates this in a limited way as: Don't work on Sundays. The way the Pharisees applied the law was too intense. If you had worked Monday through Saturday, you would not be allowed to work on Sunday. Now what if there was a woman with a baby and her husband had just died and she needed help moving? The only day you have off work to do this good deed is Sunday. So, you go to help her out. Well, the Pharisees just might show up and form a picketing line to shut you down. Moving, as you well know, is a lot of work. When Jesus would perform a healing miracle on the Sabbath, these guys would make a big fuss, and try to shut Him down as well. (More on that in the next chapter.)

When Jesus showed up on the scene, He came up against these Pharisees time and again. Jesus tried to show people what the Sabbath was really for. He pointed out that we aren't supposed to work our lives away. Avoid that trap. Seven days of working each week is too much. Beyond that: Honor God in what you do, take time to pray, sing songs to God, go to church, have meals with friends and family, and spend some time doing that wonderful thing, that hobby you were created to do like fishing, gardening, or oil painting! We need time in our lives for pleasure, for "flow," and for rest. If you have to work on Sunday, make a space for some Sabbath time on another day of the week. It is a gift to God that gives back to your own soul even more. When God created the world, even He rested on the seventh day. (I have gone through a six-month season of not turning on my computer each Sunday. My computer is a hub of distractions that is running me ragged. I need a break so I don't collapse. It is so nice not to be ruled by devices at least one day a week. I'm not a puppet!)

The Pharisees remind me of the character Church Lady from the TV program "Saturday Night Live" (SNL).[2] They seem like they're looking down their noses, too holy to associate with real people. They augment God's rules with a bunch of man-made misinterpretations of God's precepts. Next, they're trying to catch people breaking these made-up policies that are way too strict in the first place. God is about our hearts, not a list of dos and don'ts.

PART 2

Jesus answered him, "Simon, I have something to tell you."
"Tell me, teacher," he said (Luke 7:40).

Jesus has been invited to a Pharisee's house for dinner. As they are eating, a woman who has led a sinful life comes into the room and pours perfume on Jesus and cries at His feet. Simon the Pharisee turns to the person next to him and says that if Jesus knew what sort of a woman she had been, He would never let her touch Him. Jesus hears him and says, "Simon, I have something to tell you." Simon's answer is perfect. Simon says, "Tell me." This makes me think he is probably a teachable Pharisee. Since it is possible that we all have an element of "Pharisee" in us, it would be good to be a teachable one!

Jesus goes on to relate that there are two people who owe money to a moneylender. One guy owes $40; the other guy owes $40,000. Neither one of them has the money to pay back the loan. For some great reason, the moneylender decides to cancel the debts...both of them. Jesus asks Simon the Pharisee which person will love the moneylender more. Simon figures the guy who owed $40,000 will love more, because he had the greater debt canceled. Jesus says, "Yup, you're right." Jesus suggests that people who have been forgiven of bigger sins will often love God more immensely. People who weren't all that bad in the first place often have a relatively smaller love and appreciation. After that, Jesus turned to the woman and said, "Your sins are forgiven. Your faith has saved you. Go and be at peace."

PART 3

"I tell you," he replied, "if they keep quiet, the stones will cry out" (Luke 19:40).

At this Pharisee moment, Jesus is about to enter Jerusalem. It is the last week of His life. He has been on the road going almost nonstop for the past three years. There have been great miracles and healings pretty much everywhere He has gone. There are many people following Him—crowds. This is Passover week in the capital city. Jerusalem is the place where everyone wants to be for Passover. Jesus comes into town riding on a donkey. It is simultaneously a humble and royal entry. There was an 800-year-old prophecy about Jesus from the prophet Zechariah saying that this was going to happen.[3] (Big thought: This is a physical demonstration; Jesus is representing Himself as the sacrificial Lamb of God *and* High Priest.) The disciples and the whole crowd are going nuts. Everywhere people are yelling, "Glory to God!" "Praise God!" "God is awesome and His miracles are great!"

And then there are the Pharisees, looking down at everyone, their lips all pursed up like dried prunes. Frankly, they are nervous and offended. They tell Jesus to tell His folks to keep it down. They say, "Teacher, scold Your disciples." Jesus tells them that it has to be this way. If the people were silenced, the rocks and stones would sing and cry out. Even nature had been waiting for the coming of the Lord. There was no shutting down this triumphant entry into Jerusalem. Humankind and nature were created to whoop and holler, and wow, and celebrate God. He's awesome. He's good. He does great miracles! Hip-hip-hooray!

It's sad to think that many of the best-educated religion scholars of the day missed God. When He showed up on the scene, they tried to shut Him down. Beware! This is still happening today! Don't let "Pharisee Christians" block you from wanting to know more about God. And please note that SNL's Church Lady is *not* a valid representation of what it is like to know Jesus! There is sooo much more to being a friend and fan of Jesus. The Bible may look like a big book of rules to some people. But when you really get to know the character of Jesus, there is so much joy and celebration. Destiny is released. The blind can see. The dead are raised. Those paralyzed by life get to start out on a fresh new path.

Now, *"Isn't that special!"* (If you didn't follow Saturday Night Live, this is Church Lady's tongue-in-cheek tag line.) God loves our individuality and unique expression! God has perfect plans and a place for you. The word "Amen" sounds almost exactly like "I'm in!" Don't be dissuaded by Pharisaical Christians. Tell God, "I'm in!" You may have to try a few churches before you find the one where you belong. Amen.

THOUGHTS AND QUESTIONS FOR CONTEMPLATION AND DISCUSSION

Imagine playing sports (like soccer or baseball) without rules. No, I'm serious…go through the process of imagining it. What are the problems with having too few rules, or too many rules, or rules which are too strict? Look at both sides.

- Are rules such a bad thing?

- What is good about having a set of guidelines to live by?

- Are the Pharisees good people? What is good about them? What is bad about them? How could they have been more receptive to God? (So you know, there is no section in the Bible where the Pharisees stop someone from moving on a Sunday. I made that up, hoping to illustrate a point.)

- What are some dangers in pointing a finger at someone in a church or community and calling them a Pharisee?

- Is the problem in the rules, or in the heart? Or does it depend? Expound on this.

- What is the Sabbath? What is it for?

- What are some good things to do on your day off?

- How can you let God be part of this special day?

- How can doing your amazing hobby bring glory to God?

- Do you know people who seem too holy to be kind?

- How do they make you feel about God?

- How about you? Are you being like a Pharisee in any way, more interested in rules and principles than people? It might be easier to catch yourself acting like a Pharisee than you think! Jesus applied the word "hypocrite" to these guys often.

- Ever catch yourself being a hypocrite? Take another look at yourself. No, even closer, get the magnifying glass!

- What is good about Simon the Pharisee's reaction to Jesus?

- How do you react when someone corrects you? Are you ready to weigh their words? Or are you sensitive and quick to jump to your own defense? Or are you too hard on yourself? What can you do to get the best results out of a healthy critique?

- Do you feel like the person forgiven more will love God more? Why and why not?

- Why are people so excited when Jesus enters into Jerusalem on a donkey?

- Why is it good for people to celebrate and praise God?

- How does God win when we do that? How do we win?

- How has sin entering the world affected nature?

- Why would the rocks want to rejoice about God setting a restorative plan in place?

- How can Pharisaical people be damaging to the work that Jesus has in mind?

- How can "harsh religion" block God's plans?

- How does media representation of God's people block others from wanting to know more about God?

- Do you go to church? If not, try visiting several churches in your area. Ask friends which churches they like, and why they like them.

Notes: This text has been influenced by the passages of Luke 7:36-50 and Luke 19. About the story in Part 2, Matthew 26:6-13 relates a similar event, or perhaps the same scene told from a different perspective.

ENDNOTES

1. Pharisee definition from dictionary.com.

2. "Saturday Night Live," SNL Studios and Broadway Video, Lorne Michaels, NBC. Church Lady was a popular repeat character played by comedian Dana Carvey.

3. Zechariah 9:9.

TWO BLIND MEN

Jesus stopped and ordered the man to be brought to him. When he came near, Jesus asked him, "What do you want me to do for you?" "Lord, I want to see," he replied (Luke 18:40-41).

PART 1

Bartimaeus was a blind beggar who sat by the side of the road in Jericho. Being a beggar wasn't a great way to make a living, but in that culture it might have looked like that was about all he could do. One day, a large crowd came through town. Bartimaeus could feel the excitement and hear lots of noise. He quickly discovered that it was Jesus and His entourage. He started yelling and yelling and yelling, "Son of David! Have mercy on me!" People looked at him and told him to knock it off. No way! He yelled more, and louder. Jesus heard Bartimaeus and told the crowd to go get him. Bartimaeus jumped up and practically bounced his way over to Jesus—he was sooo excited! Face to face with each other, Jesus asked Bartimaeus,

"Now, what's up? What do you want Me to do for you?" Blind Bartimaeus knew exactly what he wanted Jesus to do for him that day. He confidently stated, "Lord, I want to see!" Jesus said, "Well then, receive your sight." At that moment Bartimaeus could see. He immediately dropped all his other plans. He joined Jesus's crowd that very minute, and off they went. And even though he could see, there was no "looking back"!

PART 2

There are other records of people being healed of blindness in the Bible. John 9 tells about a different man who was blind from birth. I'll make up a name for him. Let's call him Victor! Jesus and his gang came upon Victor as they were traveling. The technique for this healing was a little different from the last one. Jesus spit on the ground and made some mud with the saliva and dirt. Jesus rubbed this muddy goop over the blind man's eyes and then sent him to a special pool called Siloam to wash off the mud. It has been suggested that this man may not have had eyeballs and that Jesus was sculpting them. In the beginning of the Bible, God created man from the dust of the earth, and then breathed life into him.[1] (Boy, I thank God for my vision pretty much daily. I love seeing! If you don't have one other thing in your life to be thankful for, but you can see, start thanking God for that! Vision is amazing! Colors, textures, patterns, shapes!) The blind man did just what Jesus told him to do. Victor went to the pool and washed off the mud-spit, and he actually came home seeing! He could see! This confused the heck out of people, and even started an uproar with an unhappy surprise ending. Mind-boggling!

The neighbors didn't believe it was the same man, and Victor couldn't convince them that it was him. They decided to get the Pharisees involved. The Pharisees got right to the point. The wrong point! GAH! The Pharisees were quick to point out that this healing had been done on the Sabbath. Oh no! These overzealous sticklers couldn't understand why a Man of God would heal someone on the Sabbath. (Like duh!) That's when a whole debate started over whether or not a sinner could perform a miracle. The Pharisees decided that Jesus must be a sinner because He had done "work" on the Sabbath. Victor's parents were dragged in as witnesses. They were afraid to help out because the Pharisees had threatened to kick anyone out of the synagogue who followed Jesus. The parents pass the buck and tell the Pharisees to ask Victor what happened. So they ask Victor all the same questions, again and again. Furthermore, they want him to testify that Jesus is a sinner.

Victor gets frustrated and amazed at them and says, "I don't know if Jesus is a sinner. But, the one thing I *do* know is that *I was blind, but now I can see.*" That probably should have settled everything. Sadly, it didn't. The Pharisees threw Victor out of the town—they kicked him out for being "steeped in sin from birth," and for "lecturing" them! Yuck! Holy cow! Can you believe it? I had to reread that part, twice, it surprised me so much. These men seem to be unteachable, stiff-necked Pharisees. I hope they got a good look in the mirror before they had their appointments at Heaven's gate.

Jesus heard what had happened and gave a sermon on "spiritual blindness." The man who had once been blind was very receptive to new teaching. He was now awakening to spiritual vision as well as physical vision and wanted to know everything God wanted to teach him. Jesus was explaining to this guy that if someone is blind one minute and then can see the next minute, the person might instantaneously get a greater understanding of who God is than someone who went to church his or her whole life, but never really experienced God. "Blind" can refer to physical vision through eyes, but it also can simultaneously indicate spiritual understanding. This story continues with this 40 verse:

192 FORTIFY YOUR SOUL

> *Some Pharisees who were with Him heard Him say this*
> *and asked, "What? Are we blind too?"* (John 9:40)

Jesus didn't respond, "Uh-Duh!" That would have been rude. Jesus was often very direct, but not downright rude. Once again, Jesus was a stellar role model. He simply responded to the Pharisees by saying that before they knew the truth they might have been found somewhat innocent. But once they have been offered revelation, they'll be judged differently. In other words, if you're gonna go acting like know-it-alls when you've got it wrong, and like you are "Big Stuff," watch out!

God likes when people stay humble and teachable. He'll be teaching us new fabulous things for our whole lives. We'll never be master of all wisdom and knowledge. These Pharisees were supposed to be leading people *to* God. Instead, they were blocking people away from Him, and they were going to end up accountable for what they had done. In this case, false authority equals guilt. Self-righteous, phony, and hypocritical behaviors usually become uncovered. That may be one reason I am getting a little nervous about writing this book. Now that I have set myself out there as someone who knows something about Jesus and the Bible, and I am stepping out to share it with others, I have to try to live at the standard I have put forward in this writing. That feels intimidating, and very challenging, and yet I keep writing. *Gah! Help me Jesus! I can't do it without You!*

THOUGHTS AND QUESTIONS FOR CONTEMPLATION AND DISCUSSION

In the ever-popular song "Amazing Grace," we sing, "I once was lost but now I'm found, was blind, but now I see."

- What does blind mean in this song?

- When you lose your blindness in this sense, how is your life changed?

- Have you experienced this? Are you still thinking about it? (There is a salvation prayer at the end of "Chapter 40," if you want to go check it out while you're thinking.)

- Are you ever afraid of making a fool of yourself in front of people?

- What can you learn from Bartimaeus about how to get break-through with God?

- What do you want God to do for you?

- What are you afraid to ask of God because it seems too bold, or too presumptuous?

- Does Bartimaeus's request seem bold and presumptuous?

- Is God possibly disposed to do more for us than we might ask for?

- Jesus said, "Receive your sight." What does it mean to receive?

- What was Jesus offering, sight, or the potential to receive sight?

- Is it possible that Jesus could have passed by and Bartimaeus remained blind? How?

- What things did Bartimaeus do to participate with "receiving" this healing?

Think about the goopy mud-spit cure Jesus offered.

- To what extremes do people go when it comes to getting healed?

- It is certainly OK to go to doctors. God often uses medical wisdom and technology to help in healing people. Where do you turn first, to God or to doctors? When you turn to God, are you looking for a Band-Aid or *greater* wellness?

- What is the difference between these two (Band-Aid versus wellness) outlooks in our bodies, hearts, and minds? How is it possible for bad attitudes and behavior patterns to manifest as physical health conditions? (Example: rage might lead to hypertension; unforgiveness might lead to bone problems.)

- Why did the neighbors not believe Victor was the same guy?

- Why was there a big trial over it? What was the big deal?

- What was important to the Pharisees?

- Why were Victor's parents afraid of the Pharisees? What were their choices? How is this unreasonable?

- Why didn't this miracle speak for itself?

- What is blindness?

- Who was really blind?

- Why was Victor kicked out of town?

- How did the lives and attitudes of the two guys who had experienced a miracle change, both practically and spiritually?

- How do you think your life would change if you experienced such a touch from God, a miracle?

- How did Jesus *not* treat the Pharisees when they asked what seemed like a stupid question?

- How could that question have led to a fruitful exchange and a life-changing encounter for them?

- How often does being rude, judgmental, and sarcastic block us from leading others into a life-changing encounter?

- How can we change what might be categorized as "stupid questions" into opportunities to share Good News, God News?

- What are the dangers in acting hypocritical and self-righteous? The Bible says that we will have an opportunity to be measured against our own measuring stick (Matthew 7:2). (Yikes!)

- How well do you keep your own rules? If you are anything like me, you might sometimes find yourself critiquing someone for doing something that you actually do, too. That's one of the reasons it is great to follow Jesus! He is more gentle and full of grace than most people tend to be. I'm going to make every attempt to stay humble and teachable. How about you?

Note: This text has been influenced by these passages in the Bible—Part 1: Luke 18:35-43 and Mark 10:46-52; Part 2: John 9.

ENDNOTE

1.   Genesis 2:7.

THE GREATEST COMMANDMENT

All the Law and the Prophets hang on these two commandments (Matthew 22:40).

I n Jesus's day there were two groups of religion scholars, the Pharisees and the Sadducees. They were often hanging around Jesus, watching Him closely. They could see that He had a great amount of spiritual wisdom, and they figured they wouldn't mind learning something new from Him. They would ask Him a lot of questions. But it is also pretty clear that they wanted to try to stump Him. It seems like they would just love to catch Jesus messing up, getting confused, or giving a bad answer.

Sadly, I can sort of identify with this. Before I was a Christian, I would watch Christians closely. I was curious to see if they would mess up, if they would practice what they preach. The thing I didn't really understand at that time—Christians are not perfect people. Jesus was the only perfect Person to ever to live. Christians are imperfect people who love a perfect God and are trying to "do" life well, with the help of a holy God who guides them along the way. Could I catch a Christian being hypocritical? Sure! That really isn't hard! You probably don't have to go much farther than a church parking lot after a service to accomplish that. Nailing Christians isn't interesting to me anymore. Now I want to see people keep raising their hopes and standards. Spiral upward. I want to see people released into their calling and destiny. I want to see people get bold enough to take risks, even if it means they might make a mistake sometimes because they are moving at greater levels of experimentation.

Try as they may, these two groups of guys, the Pharisees and the Sadducees, could never stump Jesus. They came to Him one time and asked Him which of the Ten Commandments is the most important. Jesus had an easy answer: #1, Love God. Then He added a bonus. #2, Love and respect others in the way you would want them to love and respect you. Treat people the way you want to be treated. All the other commandments can be boiled down to these two. I bet if you wanted to reduce the whole Bible to two sentences, these two would sum it up pretty well. The way Jesus phrased #1 is like this: "Love the Lord your God with all your heart and with all your soul and with all your mind and with all your strength" (Mark 12:30). That's a pretty tall order, but there it is, Commandment #1. But wait! There's more:

> *The King will reply, "Truly I tell you, whatever you did for one of the least of these brothers and sisters of mine, you did for me"* (Matthew 25:40).

Later in the Bible, Jesus tells of a future time when all people from all nations will be gathered before Him. He'll be separating the people who have pleased Him from the people who have not. The King, Jesus, turns to the good guys and says, "Come on into the Kingdom… for when I was hungry you brought Me food; when I needed a place to stay you gave Me shelter; when I needed warm clothing, you hooked Me up; you even visited me in the hospital, in prison."

The people Jesus was talking to didn't understand and said, "Dude, when did I do that?" Jesus explains to them that the things they did for people who were in need, they were actually doing these things for God. Now the other group who had not pleased God were banished from the Kingdom. They got upset and asked why. Jesus explained to them that even though they may have gone to church each week, they hardly ever did a loving thing for anyone. Each time they turned their back on someone in need, it was as if they had turned their back on God Himself. Sounds like the two greatest commandments all rolled into one, doesn't it? We show love to God as we are showing love toward others.

Bonus Love Lesson: A little game I play is to look at the well-known "love" section of the Bible to see how I am doing at loving other people. I usually find that I have a bit of growth ahead of me. I'm grateful to have a scale like this for measuring love. It means I can find ways to improve, to do it better. In all of the blanks in the next paragraph, the word in the Bible is referring to love. (Love is patient, love is kind, etc.) First I put the name "God" in the blank so I know the ultimate standard (God is patient, God is kind, etc.); and then I put my own name in the blank (Laurie is patient, Laurie is kind, etc.). If my name sounds ridiculous in that blank, then there is room for improvement! Here, check it out. Put your name in the blank.

_____ *is patient,* _____ *is kind.*
_____ *does not envy,* _____ *does not boast,*
_____ *is not proud.* _____ *is not rude,*
_____ *is not self-seeking,*
_____ *is not easily angered,*
_____ *keeps no record of wrongs.*
_____ *does not delight in evil,*

but _____ rejoices with the truth.
_____ always protects, _____ always trusts,
_____ always hopes, _____ always perseveres
(see 1 Corinthians 13:4-7).

These are some other signs of growing in maturity with God. God makes us good so that we can bear good fruit.

> *The fruit of the [Holy] Spirit is love, joy, peace, patience, kindness, goodness, faithfulness, gentleness, and self-control. Against such things there is no law* (Galatians 5:22-23).

THOUGHTS AND QUESTIONS FOR CONTEMPLATION AND DISCUSSION

- What is your attitude toward Christians?

- Are you a Christian?

- Why do you suppose non-Christians watch Christians to see if they will mess up?

- Why do you suppose some Christians watch Christians from other denominations or "streams" to see if they will perform well?

- Why is "love God" the number one commandment?

- How can you "Love the Lord your God with all your heart and with all your soul and with all your mind and with all your strength" (Mark 12:30)?

- What are some of the things that get in your way?

- What can you change to do this better?

- What does it mean to love and respect others as you would want them to love and respect you?

- How can you love and respect someone who clearly does not love and respect you? Or someone who does not love and respect him or herself?

- How can you show love to God?

- How do you ignore God? Think of a few extra things you can do to help out in your surroundings. Perhaps there is someone who could use help, a favor, a visit, or encouragement?

Go back over the "Love Lesson." You may have seen some version of this somewhere else. That doesn't matter. This is the kind of thing that should be done periodically. Grade yourself. Maybe each blank could be worth up to 5 potential points. See how much you can bring your score up in the next year.

Review the "Fruit of the Spirit" verse. Memorize the list. Write it on a sticky note and put it on your mirror, or the dashboard of your car, or on the fridge. Aim for growing an orchard of beautiful fruit. Keep your mind, soul, and heart set on growing fruit for God.

Do you find a text like this overwhelming? There seem to be two opposing mindsets standing on each side of this text: (1) not doing anything to help, (2) beating yourself up because you'll never be able to do enough to please God. How can you find the perfect place in between these two mindsets?

Note: This text has been influenced by Matthew 22 and 25 in the Bible.

LAZARUS

Jesus said, "Did I not tell you that if you believe, you will see the glory of God?" (John 11:40)

Jesus was friends with a family who lived in Bethany. There were two sisters named Mary and Martha, and their brother named Lazarus. I get the impression that Jesus would stop and visit these friends when He was passing through this region. Sometimes they would spread the word and a large group of people would gather and have a big church meeting. Martha was the type of woman who would flutter around making sure everything was cleaned up, then she would make coffee and snacks for everyone. If she could have it her way, she would rope Mary into fussing about with her. Mary wasn't lazy, but she knew that when you get the opportunity to hear Jesus speak, everything else can be pushed aside for a few hours.

In Luke 10, Martha is coming to Jesus and whining that Mary just wants to sit and listen to Him. She is telling Jesus that He should make Mary get back to work. Jesus says to her something like, "Martha, Martha, Martha, you get yourself all worked up over folding napkins and putting out party mix. There is something much more important going on here today. Mary has chosen what is better, and it will not be taken from her." Anyway, all that to say, Jesus had a close personal relationship with this family.

Then there arose a time when Lazarus became very sick. It was certain that he was going to die, unless maybe Jesus could come and pray for him. Mary and Martha sent word to Jesus that Lazarus was on the brink of death and Jesus should come quickly. Jesus declared, "This sickness will not end in death, instead God's Son will be glorified through it." Rather than rushing off to their friends in Bethany, Jesus and His disciples stayed where they were for two more days. These were the critical two days though, and Lazarus died.

Lazarus has been dead for four days as Jesus approaches Bethany. He finds that Martha is waiting for Him on the edge of town. She says, "If You were here, my brother wouldn't have died." She adds a faith remark that is breathtaking, "But I know that even now God will give You whatever You ask." Jesus tells her that Lazarus will rise again. She says she knows she'll be seeing Lazarus in Heaven. Jesus wants her to think deeper than this so they discuss that He, Jesus, is the Resurrection; He is the Christ; whoever lives and believes that Jesus is who He claims to be will never die. (This means a lot to somebody who believes in Jesus. To me it means that I am already living in eternity and I am never going to die. Transition to a heavenly body, yes...but my spirit will never die. *And* since I'm living *in* eternity right now, maybe I can try to live *from* eternity, and bring a taste of Heaven's goodness to the world around me.)

Next, Mary comes out to the edge of town. She says the same thing Martha said, "If You had been here, Lazarus would not have died." She is bawling her face off. Jesus aches when He sees her in so much pain. He asks Mary to take Him to the tomb. There are many people there crying and mourning for Lazarus. The shortest verse in the Bible says, "Jesus wept." It is right here, standing outside of

Lazarus's tomb. I wonder why God is crying at this moment? That is surely worth a ponder!

Jesus tells the people to open the tomb (which is a cave sealed shut with a heavy stone in front of it). Martha, always so practical, says, "The dead body has been in there for four days, guys; it's really going to stink."

It is right about now that Jesus says, "Did I not tell you that if you believed, you would see the glory of God?" Then Jesus prays, "God, I know You hear My prayers…this one is for the benefit of these people who are standing here mourning, so they can believe that You sent Me." Jesus has publicly established that He has a close relationship with the Father, and He has been sent by God. After this prayer, He turns and addresses the situation. Jesus doesn't pray asking God to raise the dead man. Instead, He directly commands the dead man to rise. Jesus declares in a loud voice, "Lazarus, come forth!"

What do you know? Lazarus comes out of the tomb. He is completely wrapped up, sort of like a mummy. The people unwrap him. He's not a walking mummy of a man, but healed and alive. I bet they had a really great celebration on that day. Jesus is the One who puts *fun* in the word fun-eral! Can you imagine? The crowd must have been blown away! Many people put their faith in Jesus on this day because they could see that He has power over death. This is not the only story of Jesus raising the dead to life, but it is probably the most well-known. I think it fits well with our "new life/fresh start" theme. Well, except for the next part—the Pharisees weren't happy about this at all. They were convinced this would create political problems. From that day on, they plotted to kill Jesus. There was now a warrant out for His arrest.

Extra FYI: In Heidi Baker's Iris Ministries in Mozambique, more than 100 people have been raised from the dead.[1] Heidi says that dead-raising is great for church growth! What a strategy! I have heard that being raised from the dead like this can really change the rest of one's life! Ya think?

THOUGHTS AND QUESTIONS FOR CONTEMPLATION AND DISCUSSION

- In what ways are you like Martha?
- How do you prioritize what is important?
- What things have begun to seem more important to you lately?
- In what ways are you like Mary?
- Why was Mary's choice better?
- What do you do when you want to be like Mary, but you have a Martha in your midst?
- How do you love and honor the Martha, but still push toward the more important thing?
- What does this statement mean to you: "This sickness will not end in death, instead God's Son will be glorified through it"?
- How could Jesus be so casual about the death of this close friend?
- Why is Martha at the edge of town and not tending to the funeral guests, being a "Martha"?
- What does it mean to be living in eternity? Have you ever thought about this?
- How should that affect one's thoughts about death?
- How should that affect one's thoughts about life?
- What might "living from eternity" look like if someone were to do it well?

- How much is possible with God?

- Are Mary and Martha being disrespectful toward Jesus?

- Are they blaming Lazarus' death on Jesus?

- How does Jesus react toward them?

- How do you react toward God when someone you love has died before you think he or she should have?

- "Jesus wept." Why was Jesus crying? Play what I call the "Well, maybe..." game. Try to come up with a few different reasons.

We never really see Jesus praying for the sick. He is usually touching them and telling them to be healed, or He is casting out demons. In this case, Jesus does pray.

- Why?

- What does He say?

- Does He pray for Lazarus? Don't say yes, look again.

- Have you heard of people being raised from the dead?

- Is it happening somewhere near you?

- Do you believe it? Why or why not?

Note: This text has been influenced by the chapter of John 11.

ENDNOTE

1. *Compelled by Love* by Heidi Baker (Charisma House, 2008), 48.

FORTY MINUS ONE

O n the night when Jesus was betrayed, He had been hanging out with His best friends having a holiday meal. These were twelve guys whom He had hand selected out of the crowds to carry His message. I'm not sure if Jesus knew exactly what was about to take place on this night. It seems clear that He had a pretty good idea, and He knew it would be awful. At the table of the great feast, Jesus picked up a loaf of bread, gave thanks to God, and told everyone (including us) to think of His body when they break open their bread to feed their bodies each day. He said, "This is My body." He ripped the bread open and passed it around. Then He thanked God for the wine and offered it to the group, telling them that the wine is His blood, poured out for the forgiveness of sin.

Jesus knew that one of the twelve guys would leave the dinner table and go sell Him out to men who wanted to kill Him. Jesus told His buddies, "One of you is going to betray Me." They were all shocked and asked Jesus, "Me? Surely not me?" Isn't it intriguing that so many of them wondered if they might be the one who would betray Him? Furthermore, it wasn't even obvious to the group that the guilty person was probably Judas! The betrayer blended in with the crowd perfectly. Jesus pointed out that it would be better for the person who betrays Him to have never even been born. This would be a serious execution, this betrayal.

Judas took the communion bread, and as he ate it, satan entered into him; the Bible says this, point-blank. Judas then left the party and turned Jesus in for thirty pieces of silver. When he told the bad guys where to find Jesus later that night, he also said, "You'll know which one is Jesus because I'll greet Him with a kiss. That'll be your clue."

Meanwhile, Jesus and a few of His favorite friends went to pray at the Garden of Gethsemane. Jesus tells Peter, John, and James to guard Him while He goes off for a few minutes to pray. They said they would, but then they all fell asleep instead of guarding Him. (I discovered an intriguing "40" coincidence right here. In three books of the Bible, this part of the story falls on the 40th verse: Matthew 26:40, Luke 22:40, and Mark 14:40.) When Jesus tells you to keep watch, don't fall asleep! Falling asleep when you are supposed to be on lookout can have drastic consequences. Jesus looked upon the sleepers and said, "The spirit is willing, but the body is weak."

Anyway, Jesus goes back to praying His heart out to God. Jesus is telling God that He would rather not suffer and die. He is asking God if there is any other way to get the job done. He says, "I want to stick around longer, but not My will, God, Your will be done." Jesus is in such anguish that He is actually sweating blood. Drops of the Redeemer's blood fall on the dirt floor of the garden. An angel comes to comfort Jesus and give Him courage. That must have been powerful!

Just then Judas shows up with armed guards and Jesus is "betrayed with a kiss." Something quite fabulous happens next. Jesus asks the guards, "Who are you looking for?" They say, "Jesus of Nazareth." He answers, "I AM He," and everyone falls over. What is so cool about this? "I AM" is a name for God. Jesus is saying, "I am God." As the power of God hits the captors, they fall down powerless. Jesus is demonstrating to the enemy forces that they actually have no power to take Him captive unless He goes voluntarily.

Another awesome thing happens here. Defending Jesus, Peter cuts the ear off of one of the armed guards who came to arrest Jesus. Jesus stops Peter from fighting and prays for this enemy guard, and his ear gets healed immediately. The ear-guy's name is Malchus. I'd bet anything that his name is recorded because he became a follower of Jesus after this miracle. Next, Jesus leaves with the guards, willingly. It was part of the deal He had made with God when He said, "Your will be done."

Jesus is taken off to endure an illegal trial that is stacked against Him with all false evidence and twisted-up testimonies. The trial has several parts: religion, politics, and popular culture. Jesus gets whipped, I mean literally. The flogging is called "forty minus one"— 39 strikes. The Roman whip of the day is not one long leather strap like the kind Indiana Jones carries. It is a particularly vicious instrument of torture. It has pieces of glass and metal in it. If you can imagine that the whip had fish hooks, lead sinkers, and exacto razor blades attached to the whip strands, that'll get you closer to the reality of this whipping. Each time the whip hit His back, it would slash, pummel, and pull away pieces of His flesh, then His muscles next. The brutes who were handling Him were also hitting Him with clubs on His face and head, and punching Him. They spit in His face, too. Then He was mocked and ridiculed, psychological torture. Next came the crown of thorns. These weren't little rose thorns, but more like 1.5 inch nails that were driven into His skull.

Jesus was then sentenced to death. He was made to carry a cross that was as heavy as a tree. He kept collapsing beneath the weight. The guards beat Jesus and made Him pick up the cross and go farther. The whole town was gathered to watch and jeer. When He couldn't possibly go any more, a guy was pulled out of the crowd to carry the cross for Him. He was Simon of Cyrene. Simon had come from Africa for Passover. (Passover is very closely related to Easter.) This ruined Simon's holiday. He was smeared with Jesus's liquefied flesh, and was now ceremonially unclean for the holiday he had traveled thousands of miles to attend. Later in the Bible we learn that Simon of Cyrene took the message that "Jesus is God" back to Africa, and his children became Christian church leaders. Simon's day was ruined, but his life was simultaneously transformed. Cool, huh? Relative perspective.

Jesus was then nailed to the cross and left to die, mostly naked. Only one of those twelve chosen guys from the beginning of this letter was with Jesus as He suffered and died. The rest were hiding, scared for their lives.

And so it came to pass that Jesus's body was ripped open, a bloody pulp, just like that loaf of wine-soaked bread. This "40 story" is nauseating and brutal. It shows man at his very worst—killing God. Jesus was God and was sent to earth to live as a human. He was the only pure and completely innocent human to ever live. For the whole rest of my life, I will never be able to get my mind around this. If I can imagine the worst things I have done, said, thought, and felt, well…those things put Jesus on the cross. The great news is that I can trust that they are in the process of being reversed, forgiven, at this "forty minus one" moment, 2,000 years before I was born. Jesus's blood was shed to erase sin, our bad mistakes, mine and yours. Jesus's body was broken so our bodies can be healthy. I believe that the crown of thorns penetrates right into our minds for healthy thoughts and balanced brain chemistry. When Jesus died, He said, "It is finished." He had completed what He had come to do.

You may wonder why Christians celebrate the cross. It seems so bloody and brutal. But it is a divine exchange. God was brutalized so that humanity can be free of the penalty of judgment for committing actions that would separate us all from God forever. It is very complex, but very simple. The smartest person can study this exchange for the rest of his or her life and keep learning new things. The most basic person can accept that this is a good deal and live within the blessing. If you've heard of people making agreements and signing them in blood, this is the ultimate version of that. This supersedes and overrides *all* other blood covenants. Even selling your soul to the devil can be canceled in a heartbeat. If we simply accept this deal, we have an agreement with God guaranteed with His own blood.

Bonus contemplation: I end up wondering about Judas. The Bible says that he was filled with remorse when he realized what he had done. He totally lost it. He threw the "blood money" back at the guys who had paid him off. Then he went and hung himself. His body fell from the tree and burst open; his guts poured out all over the ground. Most people will say that Judas went straight to hell. After all, it is written that satan entered into him. Jesus said that the consequences of his betrayer would be worse than if he had never even been born. My heart aches for Judas. I hope there is a "holy loophole." I pray that in the millisecond between when he hung himself and when he died...oh, I hope his soul cried out for forgiveness from Jesus.

I know that in the very last moment of our life we can be saved, even if it looks totally impossible. With God, *all* things are possible. No matter how badly we have lived, even unconscious in a dream we can say "yes" to the work Jesus did on the cross. But I gotta tell ya, it would be a real shame to wait until the last minute: (1) you may not have any control over the last minute of your life, and end up missing salvation for all eternity; (2) it is much more fun to get close to God while we still have some quality time left to buddy up with Him on earth. God makes such a great Friend! You don't want to miss out on this one-of-a-kind relationship!

THOUGHTS AND QUESTIONS FOR CONTEMPLATION AND DISCUSSION

This text relays that the wine represents the blood of Jesus that is poured out for the forgiveness of sin.

- What does that mean?

- And just as important, but different, what does the bread do? See Psalm 103:3, and Isaiah 53:4-5.

- Do you ever wonder if you would betray or deny Jesus? If your life was on the line and you had to choose Him and die, or deny Him and live, what do you think you would do? Although it is not common in America, in other nations people get physically tortured for becoming Christian. Some are dismembered, and even executed.

- Why would it be better for the person who betrays Jesus to have never been born?

- How is it possible that none of the other apostles saw this betrayal coming?

- What does the expression "the spirit is willing, but the body is weak" mean to you?

- Have you ever experienced something that relates to this? There were consequences here. How can you strengthen yourself to come through times of weakness better than these guys did?

- How did Jesus handle the moment of His greatest agony?

- What can we learn from this?

The Bible tells us that the enemy guard whose ear was cut off was named Malchus.

- What do you suppose happened to his perspective that night?

- How can a face-to-face miraculous encounter with God change the mindset of one who starts out completely opposed to Him?

- Was Jesus taken to the cross against His will?

- Did He deserve to die?

- What is the value of this terrible event?

- Why was He sentenced to death? By whom and for what reason?

- My favorite question: Who was *really* on trial that day?

Simon of Cyrene was just a random guy in the crowd who was selected to be a representation of "carrying the cross," or perhaps the message, of Jesus.

- How has that sort of thing happened, or tried to happen, in your life?

- Has God been trying to pull you out of the crowd for some reason? Examine this.

- What parts of the brutalization and death of Jesus for your freedom have gotten clearer to you recently?

- How is this influencing your thoughts, health, and lifestyle?

In the last chapter, Jesus raised Lazarus from the dead. Compare some thoughts about Lazarus living versus Jesus dying.

- Why did Jesus have to die?

- Is Jesus dead or alive today?

- How about you; are you dead or alive? (That is almost a trick question, if you can't answer it now, save it for later.)

- What are the benefits of not waiting until the end of your life to get to know Jesus?

Note: This text has been influenced by these the chapters of Matthew 26–28; Mark 14; Luke 22; John 18.

PART V

OLD TESTAMENT—CAPTIVITY AND RESTORATION

JOASH

One of the interesting things about writing all theses "40 stories" is that I am not completely familiar with all of them. I have been spending a lot of time digging through the Bible, asking God questions about these personalities and scenarios. This is certainly the case with Joash. I started out not knowing a whole lot about him. I had him confused with a guy named Josiah. I had to do a lot of reading and re-reading to understand this story. Originally, all I saw was the number 40. That was how I chose to write about Joash. When I saw that Joash reigned for 40 years, I was influenced to conclude that he was probably a pretty good king, overall. I started with an assumption that the nation of Judah (AKA: God's people) would be in better shape at the end of his reign than when he started. However, there is a bit of a twist in the end of his 40-year reign.

To overly simplify things, we could say that Israel had a civil war and broke into two separate nations: Israel and Judah. In the history of Israel and Judah there were good kings and bad kings. Ahab and Jezebel were among the very worst rulers. You have already read about them a little bit in the Elijah story. Israel was overrun with witchcraft. It was a terrible, wicked place to live while they reigned. When Ahab died, his descendants became next in line as kings, and they were continuing in these very bad ways. Judah and Israel both end up entwined in this particular evil season. Ahab and his sons were kings in Israel. But the king of Judah, named Ahaziah, was related to Ahab through marriage.

Eventually God decides that enough is enough. This evil influence will not be changed without serious action. God overrides the decisions of men, and He installs a new king. Jezebel gets pushed out of a window by her own eunuchs, then trampled by horses, and eaten by dogs. There is no grave site for her memorial. In addition, all the male descendants of Ahab, sons and grandsons, are put to death. Seventy of them. Even King Ahaziah of Judah, the one related through marriage, is killed. Then there is a backlash of the bad guys retaliating. It is a very unstable time in both Israel and Judah.

In this confusing uproar, there was a baby prince named Joash who was supposed to end up dead. He was the son of King Ahaziah, but he does not appear to be related to Ahab. During the retaliatory uproar, an aunt grabbed this baby Joash, and saved him from being slaughtered. All the rest of the royal princes were killed. Auntie kept him in hiding in the temple for six years while the country was upturned. (Imagine being able to hide a little boy in a temple for six years, undetected. That is interesting to me.)

When it finally became safe to bring Joash out of hiding, he was enthroned as the rightful heir of Judah. He became king at the age of seven. That must have been so cute. Imagine his little crown and miniature throne! The chief priest of the nation, Jehoiada, had a lot of influence at this time. He had Joash and the whole country dedicated to following God, interested in being God's people. Jehoiada was a very good and godly man, a good influence.

The worst of the enemies have been killed and a fresh season of safety begins. The people tear down most of the altars to Baal, and clean the idols out of God's temple. In fact, the big project that Joash is involved in during his reign is restoring God's temple. He takes a money collection and distributes it to the priests so that repairs can be made. When it becomes clear that things aren't getting done as well or as fast as it seems they should, the money is distributed directly to the carpenters, stonecutters, and other laborers. The "regular guys" who come to church often do a lot to build up God's house and help His Kingdom advance. In this case, the resources are being put into the hands of the people who are the most effective at getting the job done.

As long as Chief Priest Jehoiada advised Joash, Joash did a great job of leading the country. A good mentor is vital—the difference between success and failure can often lay in the choice of who we listen to. The bad news is that Jehoiada eventually died (at the age of 130!). At this time, other officials came to King Joash and offered to support him, only they weren't followers of God. Joash started making bad choices, wrong alliances. He stopped work on the temple and started worshiping false gods. He then led the whole country in that bad direction, too. It got so bad that God chose a prophet, Jehoiada's son, Zechariah, to warn the king and the nation that they were in danger of going the wrong way. King Joash actually ended up having Zechariah killed. That part stunned me! Eventually Joash's own officials conspired against him for killing Jehoiada's son. Then they killed Joash in his bed. He didn't even get buried in the royal tombs of the kings.

This is a case of someone who started out as a good king, and he did a good job as long as he was listening to good advice. When he started listening to people with bad ideas, he made bad decisions, and came to a bad end. It wasn't supposed to go down that way. What a shame. My opinion is that God spared Joash as a child and chose him for greatness, but Joash didn't do his part in the partnership. God won't force us into relationship with Him. We have to choose to participate in His plans for us.

THOUGHTS AND QUESTIONS FOR CONTEMPLATION AND DISCUSSION

- What patterns have you been noticing with the number 40?

- Is it a good number or a bad number?

- How would you describe the symbolic meaning of 40?

- Have you been feeling more encouraged to go into the Bible to read some of these stories in their original form?

- Which stories have caught your interest? You'll have an interesting time deciphering my interpretations from what the Bible actually says! Go for it!

- How can a king leave a good or a bad legacy?

- What influence does a "leader" have on the culture of his or her nation, or their company, or the family?

- What is good about the legacy you are leaving?

- What are some of your weak points? How can you strengthen them to leave a more favorable legacy?

- How does God override the decisions of men and women, and change the direction of an individual or a nation?

- How often do you think this happens?

- Is this something God likes to do?

- Would He rather see people showing more godly initiative?

- How much impact can an aunt, uncle, or grandparent have in the life of a kid whose world seems to be falling apart? This good influence preserved Joash for a future of potential.

- Who in your extended family could use some preserving?

- Is there anyone you know who has been preserved by a family member? How?

- How much ruling can a seven-year-old do?

- Why is it important for children to have godly guardians and influences?

- What are some things that you can do to be a good influence in your immediate surroundings?

- In this text, who took the best care of the church?

- What is the responsibility of Christians to the church?

- How can we all participate in taking better care of God's house?

- If you go to church and things aren't being done as well as they should/could be in your church, what can you do to help out? (I must add that pastors get stretched pretty thin. They need help.)

God's temple can be a metaphor for our churches, but it can also symbolize our own bodies. If you are a Christian, the Holy Spirit lives inside you.

- How should you treat this temple?

- What idols still need to be cleared out?

- How important is it to get advice from godly people?

- How do you choose who to talk and listen to?

- Do your "advisers" lead you to making wise choices with peaceful results? Or have you been wondering about the quality of their counsel?

- Is it time for a new mentor? If you have a good mentor, don't forget to thank him or her!

When Joash made decisions, it affected others beyond himself.

- How are your decisions affecting others?

- Who else are they affecting? Family, friends, colleagues—think of specific people.

- How can you leave a more godly legacy?

- Are you doing your part in your partnership with God? Why/why not? How/how not?

- What more can you do?

- What have you neglected?

- What are you doing well?

Note: This text has been influenced by these chapters in the Bible—2 Kings 9, 11–13; 2 Chronicles 22–24.

ISAIAH

When Isaiah was called by God, he was given a perfect vision of God seated on His throne. God was completely glorious—the train of His robe filled the whole room. Above Him six-winged seraphs (a type of heavenly being) were hovering in flight. They were saying, "Holy, holy, holy is the Lord Almighty; the whole earth is full of His glory." At the sound of their voices the doorposts and thresholds shook, and the temple was filled with smoke. Isaiah couldn't take it. He was overwhelmed. He knew that even though he had been a pretty good guy, when he was right there in front of God, he felt dirty in comparison. Those tiny things he would say and do that used to seem OK were now clearly profane as he stood in God's presence.

He shouted out, "I'm ruined, as good as dead now...I am a man with unclean lips, and I have seen God." At that, one of the seraphs grabbed a hot coal off God's altar and flew over to Isaiah and touched his mouth with the searing hot coal and pronounced, "All the impurity has now been burned out of you." In the background Isaiah can hear God saying, "Whom shall I send? Who would be willing to go on a mission for me?" Well Isaiah was just about jumping out of his skin. He shouted out, "Here I am! Oo-oo-ooh! Send ME!" He didn't even know what he had volunteered for. All he knew is that he had a supernatural experience with God, and now he would do anything for this truly holy, mind-blowing God. Anything!

Well, it turns out that the people of Judah are following the false gods, again. They are having their palms read and checking their horoscopes each day instead of talking to God and then listening for Him to speak back to them. They worship and adore their money and big houses. They are all full of themselves, acting arrogant and haughty. They are buying themselves the very best of everything and leaving people to starve on the streets. God hates this stuff.

Like so many of the prophets, Isaiah has been called to the tough task of letting the people know that they should adjust the way they are living. Man, does anyone ever want to hear this stuff? Who wants to be corrected by someone? Eventually these people are going to be dragged off by the Babylonians and taken into captivity in Babylon. But they can't see this clearly. Isaiah, however, has been given a good glimpse of what it will look like. Isaiah warns the people that instead of wearing perfume, they won't be able to bathe properly. They'll be so dirty they'll get sores. Instead of fancy scarves, they'll wear potato sacks. Instead of the latest hairstyle, their heads will all be shaved, women and men. Instead of makeup they will be branded by hot irons. Bracelets will be replaced with shackles. All the food and water sources will dry up and they'll be lucky to get anything at all to eat.

Isaiah is trying hard to convince these people that they don't want to go there. Isaiah's God-glimpse has shown him that these people will end up in worse shape than the poor people they had left starving in the streets—unless they turn toward God. A few simple changes could save so much grief.

There is another half to Isaiah's message that makes him considered one of the very greatest of all the prophets of God. He gets a very clear understanding of who the Messiah is to be. Seven hundred years before Jesus was born, Isaiah could see that Jesus would come to serve humanity and that He would be crushed and would bleed so that through Him all people could have access to freedom, truth, and health. Isaiah could see that the Christ would be a sacrifice, a spotless lamb. Then Isaiah could see beyond that, into a farther future when all things on earth would be made new—new heavens and a new earth. All humankind would then bow before the Lord. Every knee would bow to Jesus the Christ, whether they had followed Him and believed in Him, or not.

In chapter 40 of Isaiah's writings, he is looking into the future when Israel would be released from the captivity he was currently trying to prevent them from going into in the first place. He is speaking about something 170 years into their future. Isaiah sees that God wants to speak softly to His people in this destined day. God notices that at this long-off time they are finally humble and ready to receive Him. He will repay them double for all they have lost. In the same sentences Isaiah is using to describe what will happen in 170 years, he is simultaneously declaring what will happen in 700 years. He says that there will be a voice calling out, "Prepare the way for the Lord!" Well, that is exactly what happens when John the Baptist comes on the scene.

In Isaiah chapter 40, God brings up a few interesting questions: Who can measure all the oceans in His hand? Who can put the earth in a basket? Where does God go when He needs advice? Who can put Mount Everest on His bathroom scale? Who carries all of the people in the whole world in His arms, holding them up close to His heart? Who is equal to God? God knows that He is the answer to all of these questions. He asks us questions because He desperately wants us to come to at least a basic understanding of who He is. God is everlasting, and He never gets tired. He created all of the galaxies, the suns, the moons, the stars, and little tiny planet Earth, too. Those who put their faith in God will get fresh, new strength. They will soar on wings like eagles. They won't get worn out and exhausted. What a great 40 chapter. I like knowing that this omniscient God who is the Creator of all time, space, and matter has the heart and the strength to help us. He will even restore to us more than what we had lost, when we are finally ready to receive it.

Jewish and Christian traditional teaching both indicate that Isaiah died as a martyr for God. (It is in the Apocrypha and Pseude-pigrapha of the Old Testament. It is not directly in the Bible.) It is said that he was sawn in half with a wooden saw. He was willing to die for what he believed in. He had seen God seated on His throne in Heaven. Isaiah met God in His glory, and he was never the same again, unto death.

THOUGHTS AND QUESTIONS FOR CONTEMPLATION AND DISCUSSION

- Have you ever had an experience of being in God's presence?

- Would you like to have an experience like Isaiah had visiting God's throne room? Why?

- Talk to God about your thoughts and desires, and listen for His response.

- Why was Isaiah afraid he was going to die when he saw God?

- What made him feel that he was "a man of unclean lips"? Have you ever experienced something like that?

- Have you ever made a permanent improvement in your behavior? How?

- Do you believe that impurity can be supernaturally removed in an instant? Explain your answer.

- Why did Isaiah's supernatural encounter change him for the rest of his life?

- If you had a supernatural encounter with God, how do you think your life would change?

- What is the problem with checking your horoscope and getting your palm read?

- What else could you put on this list of spiritual activities that are not pleasing to God?

- Christianity is truly not without its supernatural edge! What are some godly alternatives to the occult?

- Do you like to be "corrected"?

- How do you take "correction"?

- What is the difference between criticism and "constructive criticism"?

- What is a responsible way of handling correction?

- How can you discern good suggestions from bad suggestions?

- What are these "glimpses" that Isaiah the Prophet keeps getting? I recommend three books, just in case you want to read more about prophecy: *The School of Seers Expanded Edition: A Practical Guide on How to See in the Unseen Realm*, by Jonathan Welton (Destiny Image Publishers, 2013); *User Friendly Prophecy* by Larry Randolph (Destiny Image Publishers, 1998); *Basic Training for the Prophetic Ministry* by Kris Vallotton (Destiny Image Publishers, 2007).

"A few changes could save so much grief."

- What things in your life come up to the top of your mind as you read this Isaiah text?

- Why would God desperately want us to know who He is?

- As you read these chapters and questions about God, what new things do you learn about His nature and stature?

- What new revelations are you having about God this week?

- What is this fresh new strength that God gives to those who put their faith in Him?

- How can you feel your soul lifting as you study these chapters?

- Why are so many of these Bible characters willing to die for what they believe in? Try to come up with at least three unrelated reasons.

- What is at the core of their value system?

Note: This text has been influenced by these chapters in the Bible—Isaiah 2 through 6; Isaiah 55 and 65; Isaiah 40.

JEREMIAH

Jeremiah served as God's mouthpiece for 40 years. But when Jeremiah spoke, nobody listened.[1] He is known as "the weeping prophet." His message started out being pretty simple: "You guys are going the wrong way. Turn around and head toward God. If you keep going the way you're going, it's gonna get ugly." He tells this to his friends, his neighbors, the people at work, and the people out on the town. Nobody listens. Next, Jeremiah talks to the local police force, then the local government. Still nobody listens. He's not a popular guy. Who wants to hear that they're heading toward trouble? This is a story of fair warnings and consequences.

Jeremiah goes to the capital city, and it can only be God's will that he ends up getting to talk to the king. The *king!* He tells the king that the whole country is going in the wrong direction. This is their fair warning. Turn the country around or something bad will happen. The sad news is that when people are going in the wrong direction, they can't see it, and they don't usually want to turn around. The wrong direction has the illusion of being harmless and more interesting than a better direction would be. Unfortunately, the wrong direction has negative consequences in the long run.

Over time, God's message to the people gets harsher. "Turn toward Me or there is going to be a major blowout. Everyone in the whole country is going to end up as prisoners." God tells Jeremiah to write his message down and submit it as an official document. Get this, the king actually cuts it up with a knife and throws it into a fire. He doesn't even consider the fair warning. This is like burning the Word of God. There will be consequences for being so brazen.

How sad to be the guy who brings the bad news. For Jeremiah, the future brings time in hiding, time in prison, time in chains, and then dragged off as a prisoner of war. He also gets thrown into a well, a cistern actually. It was almost dry. There was just a layer of mucky goop in the bottom a few feet deep. Jeremiah sank into the mud and got stuck in place for a while. Yuck. Stuck in muck up past his knees. (Ya know, I wonder how he went to the bathroom? Yup, I think about things like that when I'm reading the Bible. Just keeping it real! Don't you?)

Jeremiah had had the good sense to make a handy dandy Xerox of that official document that was burned, just in case! Next, there's a new king who asked to speak with Jeremiah, in secret. At last, somebody would listen.

Unfortunately it was sort of too late. At times like this, God can lighten the punishment, but often we still have to live with the consequences of bad decisions. That was the case for this nation called Judah. Jeremiah explained to the new king that the Babylonians were going to come in and take prisoners. (Interesting fact: In modern geography, Babylon is now Iraq.) If Judah cooperated, many people would live to fight another day. It would be a long way off, but the nation would be preserved. If they fought, they would all be killed and everything would be burned to the ground. Think about it. It has to almost look as if Jeremiah is a traitor and wants to sell out his country to the bad guys. The government doesn't really trust him. (That is why he's shuffled through prison, chains, and the mud pit.)

The new king does trust Jeremiah, but only secretly. This king is straddling the fence. He wants the good things of God, but won't stand up for Jeremiah publicly.

It finally happened like Jeremiah had been telling them for so many years. Ack! If they had only listened to him, or Isaiah over 100 years before him, they'd be free. But no! Jerusalem was overthrown by Babylon. The people who cooperated were taken captive. Much of the city was burned down. The new king's children were killed right before his eyes, and then the Babylonians gouged the king's eyes out. God kept His hand on Jeremiah, though. The Babylonian king, Nebuchadnezzar, told the Imperial Guard to take care of Jeremiah. It turns out that Babylon had respect for fortune-tellers and magicians. They figure a prophet of God is the same thing. (A common mistake.) They were wrong, but God used the mistake to His benefit. The Babylonian Imperial Guard protected and preserved Jeremiah.

While the nation of Judah was taken captive, Jeremiah was set free (in chapter 40). He could have gotten a powerful position in Babylon, but he would be hated by the Jews. Instead, he chose to stay behind and help out in a refugee camp in Judah. Some of the Israelites were rejected as captives because the Babylonians decided they were worthless. Jeremiah didn't agree. (Altruistic like you, right Dude!?)

It is a shame that Jeremiah had such a hard life. As I take a closer look at him, he seems like a really cool guy. He wanted people to have the best life they could. You know, he wanted what was best for them, to keep them out of prison. It cost him much as he tried to save them from themselves. It's not like he was a narc or a nag. He had a serious warning that could have saved the whole nation from losing everything. The assignment God gave Jeremiah was tough. He put the needs of others in front of his own comfort, repeatedly. I bet he gets a really nice house in Heaven, for all eternity, as a reward for his obedience and faithfulness to God!

THOUGHTS AND QUESTIONS FOR CONTEMPLATION AND DISCUSSION

Remember a time in your life when you were warned about something that would probably go wrong if you behaved a certain way.

- What did you do with that information? What happened?

- Why is it so hard for people to see clearly when they are heading in a bad direction?

- What is going on in the spiritual realm?

- How does the enemy get us started down a bad path?

- What are some of his techniques?

- How does he keep us blinded, or captive?

- How convinced was Jeremiah that he had an accurate warning from God?

- How far was he willing to go to see people remain free?

- What were some of the personal prices he paid for people who had no desire to listen to him, and probably even made fun of him?

- Have you ever been in a similar situation? What did you do?

- Would you do anything differently having heard Jeremiah's 40 story?

- What are some of the similarities between Isaiah's and Jeremiah's ministry?

- What differences do you notice? When did they live? See the time line.

- As you read the Bible stories, do you get quirky questions, like how did Jeremiah go to the bathroom when he was stuck in the mud up to his knees? How might these quirks be useful for drawing you deeper into the stories?

- What is the difference between the fortune-tellers and the prophets?

- Why didn't Jeremiah go to work for the Babylonian government? Would that have been wrong by God's standards? This might be a trick question!

- What does altruistic mean? Consider the differences between healthy and unhealthy versions of altruism.

- What was cool about the kind of person that Jeremiah was?

- What do you find that you like about him?

- What is the difference between being a cool prophet and being a narc or a nag?

- Would you say that Jeremiah was a success or a failure? Why?

- What would popular culture say?

- What would God say?

- By whose standards would you like to be measured?

You are getting closer to being finished with this book. It is time to start looking for what you will do next to get more of God. I always like to have my next book waiting for me. See the list of resources at the end of this book for some good ideas.

Note: This text has been influenced by Jeremiah 36 through 40.

ENDNOTE

1.   *NIV Life Application Study Bible* (Tyndale House and Zondervan, 1988–2005). Study Guide Introduction to Jeremiah, page 1186.

NEHEMIAH
AND EZRA

I n the Isaiah and Jeremiah histories, the people of Judah are being
warned that they will be taken into captivity by Babylon if they
don't get their acts together. It turns out they didn't get their acts
together and they ended up captives. Centuries later, in the Nehemiah
history, the Jewish population has finally been released from this captivity in Babylon. They are starting out fresh and have been trying to
build brand-new lives among the ruins and to restore Jerusalem.

Nehemiah is one of the Jewish men who has been in exile in
Babylon. He was impassioned to hear the report about how his home-
land had survived. It was suggested that the city of Jerusalem was in
very bad shape. The walls and buildings were knocked down and
overgrown with weeds. Also, the people who had been left behind,
and those resettling the land, were being seriously oppressed and bul-
lied. Some folks had gone to see the condition of Jerusalem and they
brought a report back to Babylon, to the king of Babylon. Nehemiah
was still in Babylon, working as the cupbearer to King Artaxerxes.

Nehemiah was considered to be a very honest man. His job was to
protect the king from being poisoned. In this position he also heard

a lot of private conversations. As Nehemiah served the king his wine, he was very sad and distracted by the news about Jerusalem. The king had never seen this intelligent, professional man look so down, so he asked him what was going on. Nehemiah told King Artaxerxes that he wanted to take an extended journey to help rebuild Jerusalem. Artaxerxes not only let him go, he also sent Nehemiah off with (1) letters of recommendation to the local governors, (2) a cavalry for protection, and (3) resources for the building project. Nehemiah was equipped with authority, power, and resources to get the job done.

The local officials in Jerusalem were named Sanballat and Tobiah. They were not happy to see the arrival of someone who had come to promote the welfare of the Israelites. Plus, King Artaxerxes had given Nehemiah official authority that superseded both Sanballat and Tobiah. For three days Nehemiah kept a low profile. He didn't tell anyone that his heart's desire was to get everyone organized to rebuild the city wall and gates. He went out on the third night to inspect the damage. It was very extensive, but he was not intimidated. After assessing the damage, Nehemiah came up with a plan and gathered the Jews, the priests, the nobles, and the officials. He told them that God and the king were both on his side. Then he encouraged every-one to get started rebuilding the walls. It was a huge project, almost overwhelming! Sanballat and Tobiah came around to mock, under-mine, and intimidate them. Nehemiah pointed out that he and his people had historic rights to this land. Nehemiah stood his ground, and brought a lot of morale and encouragement to the Israelites.

My favorite chapter in this book is chapter 3. Everyone has gath-ered together regardless of their family background, social status, and occupation. They all stand side by side and rebuild their shattered lives as a united team. The lawyers are standing with the garbage men. The hairdressers are gathering stones and handing them to the pastors. The contractors are working with the pharmacists and the artists. Everyone starts working on the portion of the wall closest to their homes. When people would finish their assigned section, they would help the people who hadn't finished yet.

Meanwhile, the enemies gathered to make the Israelites' lives more difficult. They would yell things like, "You guys are so bad at building walls that if a fox, a cat, or even a bird were to land on it, the whole thing would fall down." It sounds like harmless taunting to me, but over time, the insults were starting to wear down the Israelites. Their motives and the quality of their work were being attacked. They were tired, too. When the bad guys saw that they were getting to them, they cranked up the harassment even more and started to threaten the Israelites physically. This is when it became very important to have a strong leader with a good plan. Nehemiah kept all his people working in unity. The Israelites took turns guarding each other while they were working and sleeping. The threats got so serious that the Israelites were even sleeping dressed for battle.

It took over twelve years to rebuild the city walls and gates. But, finally the huge endeavor was finished. When the enemies saw that it had been completed, they actually became intimidated. It was clear that God was helping the people who were rebuilding Jerusalem. Nehemiah was appointed to be the governor in Jerusalem. The local folks came to him with lists of problems. He would listen and try to help everyone get to the other side of their issues. One problem was that people were being charged 40 shekels for tax. The Bible makes it clear that this was an outrageous amount and people were collapsing under the weight of the tax burden. Other people had taken out loans and had the terrible overload of extra high interest. Nehemiah put new laws in place to help these people dig out of their financial distress. He also spent a portion of his salary making sure other people were eating well. Nehemiah fed 150 people at his house. He also made an extra effort to ensure that others were set up for recovery from their difficulties.

One day, there was a huge assembly in the main square of the town. Ezra the priest brought the Bible. Instead of making a speech, he simply started reading what the Bible said. Ezra was reading many of the "40 stories" that are in the Bible, and contained in this book, too. He read about how God had set the Israelites free from slavery in Egypt. Then God stood with the Israelites for 40 years in the desert keeping them safe and fed, even when they didn't deserve it. Next God brought them into the Promised Land with Joshua. Ezra read the Ten Commandments that God had given to Moses up on the mountain during those 40 days and nights. As the people listened to the words of God, their hearts broke. They could see they were just like their forefathers. They had been breaking so many rules. They had bad attitudes and no gratitude. They noticed that once again, many people had ended up like slaves, in a form of bondage to a cruel enemy. They were aware that a lot of it was their own fault; the nature of their hearts was not pure. They didn't even know the rules anymore. They hadn't ever heard the Bible read out loud like this and understood how it applied to their own lives. They were undone. This broke their hearts.

Seeing the condition of the people, Nehemiah stood to address the crowd. He told them that this day was sacred. Everyone should go and celebrate. Nehemiah pointed out that when they start to understand the Bible, and see how it connects to their lives, they should rejoice and not grieve. Understanding God is the beginning of fruitful change. Wisdom and knowledge will follow. The people started to pay more attention to the way they lived and thought after this day. Not everything was perfect. They had to watch their hearts and minds every single day, or they would start to slide backward into their old way of thinking—stinkin' thinkin' thoughts. Of course they didn't want to slip backward! Life was more joyous now. There were walls of safety. There were gates to keep the enemies from coming into town.

God's people had a prevailing awareness of how God had stood by them and helped them get into this safe place of greater praise.

Nehemiah is a great example of one man making a big difference in the lives of many other people. What everyone else saw as ruins, Nehemiah saw as potential. He brought a message of hope and comfort to folks whose lives had totally fallen apart and helped them put all the pieces back together with structure, safety, and an appreciation for God.

Thoughts and Questions for Contemplation and Discussion

- Nehemiah had a good job working in the king's palace in Babylon. Why did he feel so connected to Jerusalem?
- I don't think Nehemiah had ever seen Jerusalem. What national, social, or spiritual connections do you have that are like this?
- How was Nehemiah equipped to begin the big project in Jerusalem?
- What personality traits did he have to join with the available resources?
- You also have access to resources. What personality traits can you join with them?
- When Nehemiah arrived in Jerusalem, what kind of approach did he have?
- Why is it important to come in and get a feel for the people and the project before making a big fanfare?

Consider how the city rebuilding teams were organized. All the members of the community were in it together. They found ways to help out, first starting near where they live.

- What can we learn from that?

- What needs to be done in the area where you are located?

- What is the role of the mockers and scoffers?

- How did they wear away at the Israelites?

- What are some of the techniques of the enemy that we can identify here?

- The enemy will also try to get you to question the quality of your work, and your motives for doing a good deed. How do you protect yourself from these attacks?

- What does it mean that God's people even had to sleep dressed for battle?

- Read Ephesians 6:10-20. What is your armor? Who do you battle?

- How many flaming darts does the shield of faith deflect? What does that mean to us today? When are we supposed to take off the armor?

- How long did God's people work to restore what was broken? Perseverance is a big key to success. How did the enemies react when the Israelites completed the project?

- What does your perseverance tell your enemies, the mockers, and the scoffers?

Nehemiah found ways to help the financially oppressed people get tax deductions and lower interest rates. If you are in a difficult financial situation, talk to your bank about consolidating your loans, and building a strategy for paying down your debts. Sometimes tax situations can be reassessed, too. Make some phone calls to your local government. Sometimes all it takes is asking! At least try! (Pray first.)

- How did the residents of Jerusalem react when they heard the Bible for the first time?

- Why did their hearts break?

- Why did Nehemiah tell them to celebrate about this instead of grieving?

- What were some of the things that made this whole scene sacred?

- How do you identify with these folks?

- After the rebuilding of the gates and walls, were the people completely safe?

- What did they have to do to remain in a good place?

- What ruins in your community might Nehemiah see as potential?

- Think of people, people groups, a neighborhood, a building, etc. What instruction or message of hope can you deliver?

Recommendations: The following two references are studies by Jack Hayford, an outstanding teacher, about the book of Nehemiah. There is a lot of information about the Holy Spirit, and how He helps us have a more fruitful life.

1. "Rebuilding the Real You: The Definitive Guide to the Holy Spirit's Work in Your Life"; as a video, this study is available online.

2. *Spirit Formed: The Nehemiah Series,* available online at https://www.jackhayford.org/store/nehemiah-pictures-of-the-holy-spirit/.

Note: This text has been influenced by Nehemiah 1 through 9.

PART VI

NEW TESTAMENT— FROM THE CROSS TO THE APOSTLES

FORTIFICATION 32

FREEDOM

Jesus was dead and buried. The people who had been following Him had to be wondering: *What happened? What went wrong? The Messiah was supposed to come and conquer.* You see, Israel was in captivity again, this time by the Romans. The Hero whom God was going to send was supposed to come and bring "freedom." They had been waiting thousands of years. They had been so hopeful that Jesus was the One...and now He's dead.

Meanwhile, Jesus's disciples (which means dedicated followers) are meeting secretly to regroup. They had left their jobs and families to follow Jesus from town to town and learn everything He was teaching. They didn't always know why they were following Him. They didn't always understand what He was saying. But, they knew that when He was talking they felt more full of hope, more alive than at any other time in their lives. Disciple Mary Magdalene went to visit Jesus's grave site. When she got there she found that the grave was open and Jesus's body was missing. She went into a panic thinking somebody had stolen His body. Mary had been at Jesus's feet the whole time He was dying on the cross. He had been a great friend to her, and she to Him. In the old days, she had been tormented by seven demons, but Jesus drove them out of her. She could now have a peaceful, healthy life because Jesus had set her free. Freedom from demonic oppression. Anyway, seeing His body was gone, she freaked out and ran back to the hiding place of the disciples.

Mary tells the disciples about the missing body. They're thinking, "No way! Impossible! It would take an army to move the boulder from in front of the tomb. Plus it was sealed shut! And it is being guarded by the Romans! Get out of here!" For some reason, Peter and John take off running to the grave site. (A funny side note: John wrote in his recording of the Jesus experience that he got to the tomb before Peter. OK, maybe he was just going for accuracy. Then again, maybe he wanted it recorded for all eternity that he could run faster than Peter! Funny to think that maybe the disciples are a little bit competitive.) When Peter and John get to the tomb, they also see that it is empty.

Curiously, the burial cloth is left lying there as if the body had evaporated, like a deflated cocoon; and the linen that had covered Jesus's head was neatly folded. An angel comes and tells them not to look for Jesus among the dead; He has risen from the dead. It turns out the Roman guards were scared when they saw the angel earlier. They seem to have passed out, and the angel opened the tomb. Now remember, Jesus still had some unfinished business with satan. The Apostles' Creed tells us that Jesus descended into hell. He got the keys of death and Hades. He also rescued the people who had been held in "Sheol" (the place of the dead) and took them to Heaven. But there is still more, and it is really cool....

Jesus still has some unfinished business on earth, too. The first person He appears to is that magnificent Mary Magdalene. She doesn't recognize Him. She thinks He is the gardener. She asks Him if He knew where Jesus is. He calls her by name, "Mary." All of a sudden she recognizes Him. She's flipping out. She totally wants to grab Him and jump up and down, yelling and whooping. She goes back to the hideout and tells the guys Jesus is alive. They're like, "What are you, crazy? Snap out of it!" Well, right about now Jesus appears in the room. At first they're terrified. They think He's a ghost. He eats some food and talks to them about what the Old Testament had predicted about His death, and has now been fulfilled. He hangs out for a while and sets them at ease, then disappears. They're bouncing off the walls in wonder.

Thomas hadn't been there, so the other disciples are then telling him all about it. Thomas just says, "NOPE! You are so full of bologna! I don't buy it! I would have to see Him and touch His scars with my own hands." Well, you know what happens next, right? Jesus appears and shows this man, now known as "Doubting Thomas," what he needed to see in order to believe He is risen. Jesus says, "OK, so now you believe; but I'm going to throw in a special blessing for all the people in the future who can believe without having to see it." Freedom from doubt.

Did you ever hear that Peter denied Jesus three times? That happened while Jesus was being tortured. Peter was convinced that for his own safety he had to say that he didn't know Jesus. He was afraid they'd "go for" him, too. (I must confess, this last sentence is inspired by my getting lyrics wrong in a song from Jesus Christ Superstar.[1] Peter was singing: "I had to do it, don't you see, or else they'd 'gopher' me." I was a little kid. This statement about gophering was scary, funny, and confusing. I figured gophering might be like a big bear hug with torturous tickling! Something that Peter would really want to avoid!)

Peter is the bold guy who had just cut off the armed guard's ear in the Forty Minus One chapter. He went from being a fierce warrior ready to die for Jesus to denying he knew Jesus, not once or twice, but three times. At the moment of the third denial, Jesus had turned and looked straight into Peter's face. I would bet that ever since then Peter felt sick to the depths of his soul, and was wallowing in guilt with no hope of ever recovering. After Jesus rose from the dead He had a special meeting with Peter. He asked Peter if he loved Him. He asked three times in different ways. "Peter, do you love Me?" Three times Peter said "yes." Peter was restored. Freedom from guilt, fear, and denial. Then Jesus gave Peter a very special assignment: "Feed My sheep." Not only was Peter restored, he was also strengthened by what had weakened him. And, he got a raise. From now on, Peter would be truly fearless, and would do the extreme opposite of denying Jesus. Totally.

The first chapter in the book of Acts tells us that Jesus hung out in the "risen form" popping in and out, talking and eating, for 40 days. He appeared to more than 500 people during this time. Jesus gave many convincing proofs that He was alive. There are even records of His life in other history books, in addition to the Bible. Jesus spent this extra time teaching these 500-plus people about the Kingdom of Heaven, His Kingdom. He told them that when He returned to Heaven, He would send the Holy Spirit to keep teaching them and guiding them (and this is still going on today). Freedom from deception.

Then, right before their eyes He started to float up, and up, and up; then Jesus disappeared. The crowd just stood there looking into the sky with their mouths hanging open. Two men dressed in purest white appeared suddenly and asked the crowd why they were looking into the sky. I'd say these two were angels, which seems to be implied. It was no longer time to stand looking into the sky for Jesus to come back. It was time to review all the things that they had learned from Jesus and become a new representation of "the body of Christ" on earth...to live as if He is coming back today...to act as if we are the light of the world!

The freedom that Jesus brings is much bigger than we can imagine. He created all time, and space, and life, and matter. He lives in Heaven and does whatever He pleases. He chooses to give us a fresh start at life and good health. Yup! My thinking is: it's a good idea to get to know Jesus and the freedom that He can bring into our lives.

THOUGHTS AND QUESTIONS FOR
CONTEMPLATION AND DISCUSSION

My MacBook dictionary tells me that the word disciple means, "a follower or student of a teacher, leader, or philosophy."

- Are you a disciple of Jesus? Would you like to be?

- What does it mean to be a disciple of Jesus? If you are not, and you are considering it, there is a simple prayer at the end of "Chapter 40."

- How have you misunderstood God's purposes and presence in a situation until a later time, and then looking back you could see things more clearly?

- When you are studying the teachings of Jesus, do you feel a surge of hope and life? What else do you feel?

- Is it OK to be competitive? When is it, and when isn't it?

- When Jesus spoke Mary's name, she recognized Him. What's that all about?

- Why is Jesus throwing in an extra blessing for those who believe in Him without needing God to prove something to them?

- Are you like Doubting Thomas?

- What do you think are some of the blessings of not having to battle doubt day in and day out?

- What happened to Peter between whipping out his sword in the Garden of Gethsemane and denying Jesus in this chapter?

- Why was Peter so afraid now?

- Why did Jesus ask Peter if he loved Him three times?

- What is the difference between what happened with Peter and with Judas?

- What are some funny song lyrics that you've gotten wrong? I know it is off topic. Just have a few laughs and then go back to the study. Laughter is good for the heart.

- Did you know that Jesus hung out in risen form and appeared to more than 500 people? How does that make you feel? Why did He do this?

- Did you know that there are records of Jesus's life and death in books other than the Holy Bible? What do you think of that?

- What kinds of freedom does Jesus bring? Review the freedoms mentioned in this text and then add what He has done for you, or people you know.

Note: This text has been influenced by these chapters in the Bible—Mark 15–16; Luke 24; Matthew 28; John 18–21; Acts 1.

ENDNOTE

1. *Jesus Christ Superstar,* Tim Rice and Andrew Lloyd Webber (Decca U.S., 1970).

THE GREAT COMMISSION

Anyone who welcomes you welcomes me [Jesus], *and anyone who welcomes me welcomes the one who sent me* (Matthew 10:40).

Jesus spent a good amount of time, before and after He died, teaching people about the Kingdom of Heaven. Heaven will blow our minds for all eternity. Heaven totally rocks! No sickness, death, abuse, poverty, insecurity, mean people, snobs, lies, boredom, addiction, war, fighting, torture…you get the picture. The mission that Jesus was on was to overturn these works of the devil, and to kick the enemy's influence out of every aspect of our lives, right here, right now. Jesus shows us how to experience a slice of Heaven on earth. Any Christian worth his or her salt has an appetite for the impossible that just won't stop. We know that our God is more than capable of the miraculous. He likes when we give Him opportunities to invade our world. We eagerly invite Him to be a part of our daily lives, and to touch our circumstances. Read on.

As I have mentioned in other chapters, Jesus spent much of His time on earth demonstrating beneficial ways of living. When His example is followed, you and everyone else can have access to better lives. He is the perfect Role Model for how to live. Everywhere Jesus goes, He releases the Kingdom of Heaven. No sickness, no leprosy, no blindness—even demonic behaviors cease in His presence.

Let's flash back in time. Jesus's followers had been having a great time watching Jesus do life-changing things. They might not have known that they were in a time of training and getting their thoughts right. Or maybe they did, and they were chomping at the bit. Eventually there came the day when Jesus told His buddies it was time for them to start doing the stuff that they had been learning from Him. He sent them out on a field trip, in groups of two. He told them, "People are like wolves; now you must stay innocent and don't be offensive, but you'd better be wise, too." Then Jesus gave His followers this assignment: "Go to the lost, confused people right here in the neighborhood. Tell them that the kingdom [of Heaven] is here. Bring health to the sick. Raise the dead. Touch the untouchables. Kick out the demons. You have been treated generously, so live generously."[1] That is to say, He told them to go and erase the works of the devil wherever they went, too.

First He sent out the twelve closest disciples. Next He sent out a group of seventy-two.[2] It was the same deal again. Heal the sick and tell everyone that the Kingdom of God is near. At the end of their field trips all the disciples came back so excited. They had found they were having a good bit of success imitating Jesus and seeing people get healed. Jesus was excited, too. He told them each time they performed a heavenly action, it knocked hot air out of the devil's big, fat, lofty red balloon. Where the enemy has less power, there is an increase in health, prosperity, peace, happiness, truth, beauty, and more.

Jesus explained to these guys what a blessing it was for each of them to get to be part of this project. For thousands of years people had been looking forward to this period of time; the time when God would come to earth to show everyone how to live. And, these guys were right smack in the middle of the action. God had made it so simple for people to come into His Kingdom that even little kids could understand it. Adults could too if they would keep things simple, and try not to overcomplicate "religion." People would have to bear in mind that God is all-powerful, omnipotent. He lives in Heaven; and He can do whatever He wants, even if it defies logic and scrambles our itsy-bitsy human brains. He doesn't even have to follow the laws of science. Furthermore, God wants to use everyone who is a follower of Jesus to do the same things that Jesus did while He was here on the earth! That is why Jesus sent the same Holy Spirit who had raised Him from the dead to live inside of those who believe in Him as Lord. Christ in us, the hope of glory! Wow! What a rich mystery to explore.[3]

OK, I'm using Matthew 10:40, and the commissioning of the disciples, to segue into a very important topic. I wanted to tell you about the part of the Bible called "The Great Commission."

> Then Jesus came to them and said, "All authority in heaven and on earth has been given to me. Therefore go and make disciples of all nations, baptizing them in the name of the Father and of the Son and of the Holy Spirit, teaching them to obey everything I have commanded you... (Matthew 28:18-20).

This is the quintessential Christian assignment—but what does it mean? Well, we're going to break it down some:

1. Jesus says that He has all authority on Heaven and earth. If He has it all, how much authority does the devil have? Think...yes, that is right...none![4] The devil tries to trick

us into giving him ground. Don't do it! The only way he can do this is by getting us to agree with him. But since we know he is a liar, we can decide to listen to God instead.

2. Then Jesus says to "go" make dedicated followers, disciples, of all nations. Does that mean everyone in the whole world? Yup. We are supposed to present the information and lifestyle of Jesus to all groups of people in the world, so they can see that God is good. Jesus is the exact representation of the Father. Christians are the body of Christ. When people see Christians, they should be getting a better idea of what God is like. (We haven't always done so well. We've made some mistakes along the way. But, we're getting better at this.)

3. Then Jesus says to "baptize" them. That means totally immerse and saturate them. But, baptize in what manner?

4. He says, "in the name of." That means "in the character of." So Jesus is essentially telling His followers to go out into the world (where the devil is a powerless renegade), and to saturate and immerse all nations with the character of Jesus, God, and the Holy Spirit.

5. As people see sickness, abuse, poverty, insecurity, addiction, mean behavior, war, and torture overthrown and reversed, they'll come to experience God's Kingdom. Next they'll want to know the King of that Kingdom.

The Lord's Prayer says, "Your Kingdom come, Your will be done on earth as it is in Heaven." This is how Jesus taught people to pray so that we invite more Heaven into our lives on earth. That is why we hear stories about how people have experienced so much power when they pray this prayer regularly. Jesus is teaching His people to spread the boundary lines of Heaven here, everywhere we go. As people receive us, they embrace God's presence into their lives and good things start to happen because the Kingdom of Heaven is within us.

THOUGHTS AND QUESTIONS FOR CONTEMPLATION AND DISCUSSION

- Describe what you think Heaven is like. What it looks like, and what it feels like!

- Do you feel it is important for you to talk to people about God, Jesus, and Heaven? Why or why not?

- Do you have an appetite for the impossible?

- What is a miracle?

- Would you like to increase the probability of seeing miracles of all sizes in your life?

- How can you set up opportunities for God to invade your world?

- What is the enemy's influence like?

- How does the Kingdom of Heaven contrast to the influence of the enemy?

- Do you believe that we are supposed to do the things that Jesus did? How does that make you feel? Is it possible?

- What does it mean to raise the dead and cast out demons? Do you know how to do this stuff? Do you want to?

- What does "the Kingdom of God is near" mean? I believe that most of my life I have had a very shallow definition of this term. I challenge you to go deeper.

- Where is the Kingdom of God? What does it look like?

- What happens when the enemy loses power?

- How can you participate in this happening where you live, work, and hang out?

- What is the difference between the way adults "do" faith, and the way children believe?

- How do people overcomplicate the words of Jesus? How does this detract from His message?

- How much authority does Jesus have?

- Have much does the devil have?

- How does the devil get power?

- How do we make disciples of all nations?

- What does it mean to saturate cultures with the "character" of Christ?

- What is the character of Jesus?

- How can we help with this commission?

Christians spend a lot of time asking Jesus to "come." All the while He is telling us to *"Go."* Be on the lookout for the ways you can be part of the Great Commission—locally, nationally, and internationally.

- How has your understanding of the prayer "Your Kingdom come, Your will be done on earth as it is in Heaven" changed recently?

- How can praying this way make you feel more powerful and significant?

Note: This text has been influenced by these chapters of the Bible— Matthew 10:1-42, The Disciples' Commission; Luke 10:1-24, The Commission of the 72; Matthew 28:16-20, The Great Commission.

ENDNOTES

1.   Matthew 10:7-8 MSG.

2. Luke 10:1-24, Commission of the 72.

3. Colossians 1:25-29.

4. Bill Johnson messages from Randy Clark Healing School, Castle Rock, Colorado, 2007. Contact: Global Awakening, 1451 Clark St., Mechanicsburg, PA 17055. Phone: 866-AWAKENING (866-292-5364); website: www .globalawakening.com.

THE "CRIPPLED" BEGGAR

I like this story. It challenges me. The events in this chapter take place after Jesus goes back to Heaven. This story is an example of men living in "right relationship" with the Holy Spirit, fulfilling the Great Commission. These guys should be role models for modern-day Christians. I'd like to think that Christianity can look like this passage. I do personally know some people who are living this way, and they are seeing good results. This is an area in which I am studying, learning, and growing. I'm a disciple. I want to do "disciple stuff"!

(By the way, although I am married to a man who is, at this moment, paralyzed and sitting in a wheelchair, I, we, do not actually know the current politically correct term for people with disabilities. This type of language changes fairly often. I called this chapter "Crippled" Beggar because that is how it is phrased in half of the Bible translations I have used. The other half called the man "lame"— which is worse! Go figure. I have no desire to offend anyone by using outdated language that is not PC. Sorry if I did for a moment there! I understand that "crippled," "lame," "handicapped," and even "disabled" are labels that can make people with disabilities uncomfortable.

That is why I decided to use the old-fashioned expression "crippled." It is clearly outdated. Quoting from a document written 2,000 years ago should allow for some antiquated language, even if the concepts within the text are relevant into eternity.)

OK...here we go. Peter and John, the two friends who had raced to see if Jesus's body had been stolen from His tomb, were on their way to the temple one day. (John probably got there first.) As they were approaching, they saw a man being carried and set down in front of one of the temple gates. He was "crippled." This guy hadn't been able to stand up or walk for his whole life. He is now 40 years old. He makes a small bit of money begging in front of the temple gate called "Beautiful." This is a very high-profile gate at the temple, a popular main entrance. As Peter and John walk toward him, he's getting into his "spare some change" position. Peter says to him, "Look at me. No, *really* look. Look into my eyes." The guy thinks Peter and John are going to give him some nickels and dimes, maybe a dollar! He looks up, hopeful. Peter says something like, "Listen man, we don't have money; we're pastors. But, we've got what you really need." Peter takes his hand and starts to pull him up saying, "In the name of Jesus Christ, WALK."

The guy's legs were healed instantly. Strength came into his legs right away. He wiggled his ankles. Then flexed his knees. He took a few steps. He jumped up and down. A crowd gathered. He started walking up a flight of stairs; he ran down; he went back up the stairs taking the steps two or three at a time. Next he's doing jumping jacks. You get the picture. It's a whole big scene. The crowd grows bigger. Peter figures this is as good a time as any to put in a plug for Jesus! I mean, look what happened when they prayed in Jesus's name! Nobody could deny what had just happened. Everyone had seen this guy begging at the Beautiful Gate for the past 40 years. Now he is completely healed. Peter shares the Good News (the Gospel): Faith in the name of Jesus (the character of Jesus) makes men strong. Many people came to believe in Jesus based on the evidence this day. What a simple message—faith in Jesus makes people strong. Wow, if I can only memorize this, I might be on to something. It's that simple. I generally try to make it bigger, more intellectual.

The city officials threw Peter and John in jail overnight. Why? I don't know. Maybe for disturbing the peace. The real problem seems to be that the temple guard officials don't like "Jesus" being preached on the streets, and they want to shut these guys down. There was a trial the next day. It seemed outrageous that Peter and John were being called to account for an act of kindness to a beggar. It is interesting to note that the judge and jury ended up being very impressed by the courage and precise speech of Peter and John. They were astonished at these "ordinary" men who had been taught by Jesus. The healed man was standing with them, so they couldn't convict Peter and John of any crime. He was a "crippled beggar" yesterday, and today a "victim" of a miracle, full of fresh hope for a new life. In the end, it was decided by the jury that nobody should speak or do anything "in Jesus's name" anymore. If the disciples would agree to this, then the whole thing would be let go.

Now think about this: If you can pray in Jesus's name and a man who was injured or paralyzed for 40 years stands up, are you going to *stop* speaking in Jesus's name? Peter and John declare that there is no way that they can keep quiet about what they have seen and heard. When someone experiences this kind of power through Jesus, they aren't quite as worried about the risks. They are much more excited about what they'll be doing with God next! The price of holding back will cost other people too much. Peter and John prayed to God right then and there that He would enable them to speak with even greater boldness and to perform even greater miracles. You can see that they're going to get themselves in trouble again, right?

The funny thing is, while the officials are trying to keep the whole Jesus thing all hush hush, the trial only made it more interesting to the public. There was a big buzz on the streets and everyone wanted to know what was going on. Five thousand people were led to Christ because of this miracle. Wait, I just said 5,000. That's a big number! And the people who were trying to sweep it all under the rug? They couldn't shut it down. They actually added publicity! The enemy accidentally added advertising. What a dumb devil.

———— ∞ ————

THOUGHTS AND QUESTIONS FOR CONTEMPLATION AND DISCUSSION

- What might "right relationship with the Holy Spirit" mean?

- What is challenging about this story?

- What radical things could we each do (you and me) with a greater measure of the Holy Spirit flowing through us? I'm excited for a big answer to this question! Like...I want to really go for this!

- What is special about the kind of eye contact Peter made with the "crippled beggar"?

- How would you describe the faith, language, and actions of Peter as he interacts with this guy?

- How can the sort of faith, language, and action displayed by Peter and John be applied in the world today?

- What do Peter and John do with the opportunity that opens up after this healing takes place?

- How much credit do they take for what has happened?

- By what power did this healing take place?

- What might be some of the reasons why Peter and John got thrown in jail?

- When an innocent Christian goes to trial for representing Jesus, who is really on trial? For what are they on trial?

- What was remarkable about the way Peter and John stood trial? How can that encourage or influence you?

- What changes had taken place in the formerly crippled beggar? Where was he?

- What do you think he'll do with his fresh hope for a new life?

- What is the big deal about doing and praying things "in Jesus's name"? In this context, name and character are synonymous.

- What is threatening about the character of Jesus? I believe that the tag "in Jesus's name" has been thrown around lightly and disempowered. Explain why the expression "in Jesus's name" should be more powerful than an "abracadabra-amen" tag plugged onto the end of a prayer.

- What do you think about Peter and John's decision not to stop sharing what they have seen and heard?

- What would you have done in their situation?

- How is your life different from theirs?

- What might their lives have been like had they stopped sharing Jesus? (I'm so glad that they didn't stop!)

- Are you inspired by their prayer for God to enable them to speak with even greater boldness and to perform even greater miracles, even after they'd been persecuted? Share your feelings.

- How likely are you to pray like this?

- Discuss whether or not God's enemies can really keep people from talking about Jesus, thinking about Him, and praying in His name?

- What big favor did the devil accidentally do for Jesus when he had God's men locked up and put on trial?

- How can God harness persecution to magnify glory?

One last thought: If this Beautiful Gate was such a popular main entrance to the temple, that would mean that this beggar had probably seen Jesus alive, maybe even several times. Why was this man not healed by Jesus? There is no solid answer to this question, it is just an interesting one to ponder.

Note: This text has been influenced by Acts 3 and 4.

STEPHEN

J esus had gone on home to Heaven. Peter and James (and the whole crowd Jesus had left behind) prayed that they would still be able to display God's power. As they would pray in Jesus's name, in His character, it sure did happen! God's power was with them! Great crowds would gather in the town square to meet with the apostles and disciples of Jesus. Sick people were brought to them, and everyone was being healed. The Bible literally says throngs of people came and they were *all* healed. I checked Acts 5:16 in six different translations—each of the translations said "all." This display of God's power ended up drawing a lot of attention. The priests got very, very jealous and had the disciples thrown in jail.

This part is fun: An angel opened the jail doors and told Peter and James to head straight back to the public square to tell everybody about Jesus and how He brings people new life. In the morning the priests and judges went to get the apostles out of jail, only to find that the jail doors were locked but the cell was empty. They sure were confused to find the apostles preaching in the town square! The jealous priests got pretty peeved and took Peter and James to the Supreme Court. The priests were hoping to have these guys put to death. Now it starts to get pretty serious. At this point, an influential priest sagaciously suggests that if God is *not* with these guys, the whole Jesus deal will die down. But, if God *is* with them, there is nothing the priests or judges will be able to do to stop the spread of Christianity. The apostles were whipped and then released. This part boggles my mind: The apostles rejoiced and praised God that they were found worthy to suffer in Jesus's name. They actually got even more bold and passionate for Christ after this event. I wonder if I would be so bold.

There is a lovely man who is part of this holy group of disciples. His name is Stephen. Stephen has been appointed to a very important job. He makes sure that the widows are being taken care of. He helps them move furniture, reach things that are too high, and he carries their groceries. He also makes sure that they can get to the doctor, and get enough food to eat. He is a big ol' softy with the face of an angel. Stephen is very well respected by the whole community of Christians. See, if all the older ladies are happy, the whole town can relax!

Stephen could perform miracles. These miracles made people wonder about Jesus and want to learn more about Him. They were like signs pointing to "The Way." The Christian population was growing like crazy. The opposition would challenge Stephen and ask him questions about why he chose to follow Jesus. When they would try to talk him out of it, he could talk circles around them. Stephen was so in touch with God that when he would talk, God spoke through him. I don't really understand why those people couldn't hear what he was saying, and wanted to try to change Stephen's mind.

When it was clear that they would never be able to change him, they got so irate that they wanted him dead. Stephen was seized and taken to trial. A bunch of these opponents gathered as false witnesses and lied under oath. The judges looked at Stephen, and to them he looked just like an angel. So they asked him to explain himself.

Stephen's "trial" goes like this: Stephen summarizes the history of Israel. This was relevant, as it was his shared history and ancestry with the priests who were persecuting him. Stephen mentions how when their forefather Moses was 40 years old his life was changed. Moses's eyes were then opened to the way the Jews were living as slaves in Egypt. Defending one of these slaves, Moses killed a man and had to flee from Egypt. Then he was in exile for 40 years. After that, Moses was called by God to free the slaves. Stephen reports how these freed slaves grumbled in the desert for 40 years, and for the same 40 years they took what God gave to them without thankful hearts, and gave nothing back to God.

He tells the "40 stories" of Joseph, Joshua, David, and Solomon. He mentions how many times Israel was threatened or taken over by other nations and set free by God. History kept repeating itself. Yet these Jewish priests still didn't get it! God had come again to set them free—to free them from their own bad attitudes and the power of sin and death. Stephen pointed out that the priests who had put him on trial cloaked themselves in religion to make themselves look good, but in reality they were mean, jealous, and full of hatred. He suggested that they actually had murder in their hearts. Stephen said that for generations their forefathers had resisted the Holy Spirit and had killed the prophets of God. Now, Stephen added, they have gone and killed the Righteous One whom God had promised to send—the Messiah!

Well, of course the miserable old priests get all sorts of furious and decide to kill Stephen on the spot. Wow! I guess they don't even notice that in this murderous moment they are proving Stephen right. Once again, because they were full of hatred, the priests were killing a man of God. They rush at him and smash him to death with stones. It sounds so brutal, but something awesome happens at this moment. Heaven opens up! Stephen is not feeling any of this pain as his body is being crushed to death. Stephen is having an experience with the whole Trinity: He is full of the Holy Spirit; he sees God in His glory;

and Jesus is standing at God's side. Stephen is such an awesome guy, truly Christlike. As he is simultaneously being murdered (martyred) and entering Heaven, he prays, "Lord, do not hold any of this sin against them." Wow...to forgive people even while they are killing him! What a saint! I can't wait to meet Stephen.

THOUGHTS AND QUESTIONS FOR CONTEMPLATION AND DISCUSSION

- How were the disciples able to display God's power after Jesus had died?

- How well were they doing it?

- What is the source of the power?

- In what ways do they display the power of God?

- What is it about signs, miracles, and wonders that draw attention to God?

- Why do you suppose the miracles and healings made the priests so terribly jealous?

- How could the priests miss seeing God in those miracles and healings?

- How do you react to miracles? Define miracle.

Angels are mentioned throughout the Bible, over and over.

- What are some healthy and unhealthy attitudes toward angels?

- Is it wrong to worship angels?

- The equal but opposite warning is that it is "ignorant" to deny the existence of angels and demons. How can you tell an angel from a demon?

- Have you ever had a supernatural experience with an angel or a demon? Both might appear to be safe and beautiful. It is important to know the difference since demons are fallen angels.

After being thrown in jail, the apostles went right back out to do the same things again. After being whipped, they rejoiced that they were found worthy to suffer for Jesus.

- What is that all about?

- What do you think you would do if you were in their place?

- Has anything been able to stop the spread of Christianity? Why is that so?

- Why was Stephen's job with the widows so important?

- The Bible has a somewhat different value system from popular culture. What are some of the most important jobs being done in your community? (Personally, I truly appreciate the garbage men and sewer guys! They should probably be paid more.)

- Why was there a bogus trial sentencing Stephen to death? This seems like excessive, deep hatred.

- What force was behind the stoning of Stephen?

- Why did Stephen spend so much of his trial talking about the history of Israel, the captivity of Israel, the priests killing the prophets, etc.?

The Bible mentions "the power of sin and death."

- What power does sin have?

- What power does death have?

- How did God help Stephen at the moment of his martyrdom?

- Have you thought about the possibility of being martyred for Christianity?

- What is your level of commitment to Christ?

- How can you strengthen yourself for times of mockery, peer pressure, and worse?

- How was Stephen able to bless and forgive the people murdering him?

- Can you think of anyone you may need to forgive, even if they may not deserve it?

- Do you know that you can forgive people without having to forget what happened and without having to trust or befriend the person who perpetrated against you? Think about that. Pray about that.

- Who was really on trial that day?

- What was the real trial?

Note: This text has been influenced by Acts 5 through 7.

SAUL BECOMES PAUL

There was an important Pharisee named Saul observing the event of Stephen's martyrdom, and giving approval to this death. Saul was acting as the coat-check, making sure that the men murdering Stephen didn't get blood on their coats. On the day when Stephen was killed a great persecution broke out against the church, and many Christians were scattered. (On a positive note, this ultimately spread Christianity throughout more of the world.) Saul would go from house to house dragging men and women off to prison. He was breathing murderous threats against the Lord's disciples as he went traveling off to a city called Damascus with the goal of collecting as many Christians as he could arrest. His goal was to destroy the church and all things classified as Christian.

Quite unexpectedly to Saul, this Damascus trip turns out to be a huge success for the spread of Christianity. Something happens on this trip that completely changes the direction of Saul's life. An overwhelming light from Heaven flashed around Saul and he fell to the ground, blind. A Voice said to him, "Saul, why are you persecuting Me?" Saul asks, "Who are You?" The Voice says, "I am Jesus, whom you are persecuting." (To persecute Christians is to persecute Jesus—not a good idea. Christians are the body of Christ.)

The guys who are with Saul carry him into Damascus. Having seen the Great Light and then waiting for three days in blind darkness, the stage is set for Saul to be saved. God announces that Saul is His chosen instrument to spread the Word, the Good News that the Christ of God has come. He adds that Saul's life would be very difficult, but fully dedicated to Jesus. Saul is a new man in an instant. He gets his sight back, and is immediately baptized.

Right away his life is changed. He goes from trying to kill Christians to trying to bring new life, true life, to all those who are not Christians. As you can probably imagine, the Christian crowd is going to need some time before they can trust Saul. They are wondering if he is faking his newfound love for Jesus so he can trap them. Saul ends up having to escape from Damascus and head for a safe place. First he must learn all the things he doesn't know about Jesus, and spend a lot of time talking to God about what his new life is going to be like. It is a time of transition and a time of prayer. One thing that is totally clear is that Saul is not the same man. Everything has changed. A man of encouragement, named Barnabus, takes Saul under his wing and eventually Saul is accepted by the Christians, even into the Jerusalem crowd, the inner circle.

You know by now that people who are forgiven of very much tend to love God very much. This is certainly the case with Saul. He sets out to travel as much of the world as he can, spreading the news that Jesus is Lord. He covers a lot of ground becoming part of each community and speaking in the gathering places. He talks to everyone: Jews, wizards, women, children, philosophers, businesspeople, millionaires, leaders, beggars, etc. In every town he tries to plant at least one church. He makes it his mission to ensure that they completely understand who God is and what He has done through Jesus. He continues to write letters to the churches he has planted as he moves along to new places. Some of these letters are in the Bible.

Somewhere along the line Saul starts going by the name Paul, and the Bible calls him Paul from then on. Around this same time, it is no longer Saul going around with Barnabus. Rather, it is Barnabus going around with Paul. There has been a shift in the leading authority. It is clear that this is just fine with Barnabus! Barnabus is an encourager and a people launcher. He helps people come into their destiny!

Paul had never met Jesus "live and in person" as an apostle, but he does get to know the mind of Christ better than almost anyone who has ever lived. He met Jesus in other very powerful ways! Paul is universally acknowledged as an outstanding and immensely influential apostle of Jesus. Paul most likely wrote at least thirteen books of the Bible. He would do anything to advance the Kingdom of God. He went from being a murderer of Christians to being a "super-apostle." God did extraordinary miracles through Paul, so that even handkerchiefs and aprons that had touched Paul were taken to the sick and their illnesses were cured and the evil spirits left them. Paul's hanky! Imagine being healed by the touch of a hanky! God is such a riot!

Paul was totally sold out for Jesus. Look what he was willing to go through for the love of Christ: He worked really hard. He was imprisoned frequently, flogged severely, and exposed to death again and again. Five times he received from the Jews the "forty lashes minus one." Three times he was beaten by the Romans with rods. Once he was stoned. Three times he was shipwrecked and once spent a night and a day floating in the open sea. He was constantly on the move, in danger from rivers, bandits, his own countrymen, Gentiles, and in danger from false brothers. He often went without sleep, and without food. He spent time freezing cold and naked.

Paul also faced daily pressure with his concern for all the churches he had planted. When he saw people weak, he hurt for them. When he saw people led into sin, angry fire burned in his gut. Paul was even bitten by a poisonous snake, and that didn't harm him. There was often a death threat on Paul, like the time when 40 guys were waiting to ambush him, but he found out and got away. That didn't hold him back. No fear! One time Paul was "murdered" by a gang and left for dead. I believe it was at that time that he was taken up to the third heaven (Paradise), where he experienced inexpressible things that no person is even permitted to talk about. (I'd bet he probably hung out with Jesus while He was there.) He ended up living. It is possible that he was raised from the dead because his work for God was not finished.

Later on he was on "house arrest" for two years, so he held church services at his house/prison. Some of Paul's letters in the Bible were written while he was in chains in Rome. Tradition holds that he was eventually beheaded under the Roman Emperor Nero. Then again, in church history some say he went on to Spain before he died. Maybe both. One thing that is for certain, Paul sailed and walked more than 3,000 miles to share the love of Jesus with as many people as he possibly could, no matter what he had to endure.

When this is your lifestyle, there is no changing your mind. There are still people like Paul who will go anywhere and do anything, even risking death, so that people can learn about Jesus and have access to new life. It's interesting that Christianity started from a small group of Jewish people who caught on fire with a love for Christ, and then spread out from Jerusalem to new regions all around the world. And this Good News is still spreading over 2,000 years later. We have a friend named Leif Hetland[1] who lives this Paul kind of passion. He travels to Cuba, Tanzania, Pakistan, and beyond sharing the Good News of the Father's love. Another awesome example of this lifestyle is Heidi and Rolland Baker of Iris Global. They have planted more than 10,000 churches in Mozambique and neighboring countries,[2] and have close to 10,000 orphans in their care (as of 2014). Another person who really blows my mind is Jackie Pullinger.[3] Her work with junkies and prostitutes in Hong Kong challenges me. What saints!

⸺⸺⸺⸺⸺ ∞ ⸺⸺⸺⸺⸺

THOUGHTS AND QUESTIONS FOR CONTEMPLATION AND DISCUSSION

Take note of how vehement Saul is toward Christianity, murderously hunting down Christians.

- Would you have thought it impossible for him to become a Christian?

- Who do you know who is very opposed to Christianity?

- How were Saul's eyes opened to seeing Jesus?

- Did God commission Saul against his free will? Explore this idea.

- How is persecuting Christians equal to persecuting Jesus?

- What does it mean that Christians are the "body" of Christ?

- What changed for Saul when he had a firsthand encounter with God?

- How can someone change his mind so intensely and quickly? I said that Paul never met Jesus "live and in person," but these verses in the Bible should be explored and discussed: First Corinthians 9:1 and First Corinthians 15:8. What is going on here?

- Describe what Barnabus must have been like. How did he launch Paul into a position that surpassed his own?

- What kind of person does this?

- How could he not be jealous when Paul passed him in ministry prominence?

- With whom did Paul share the good news about Jesus?

- What was his objective?

- How convinced was Paul that what he was teaching was the absolute truth?

- How could he "know the mind of Christ" so well, having never met Jesus in person?

- What do we learn about Paradise in this text?

- Which of the things on Paul's list of sufferings have you gone through to help someone else get rescued?

The list of things Paul went through to share wisdom about God is almost overwhelming. He would seem to be completely fearless. Try to name the one thing that Paul did fear. Hint: See Psalm 111.

- How did Paul spend his time as a prisoner?

- What can you learn from this to apply to your own life? Consider: Prison isn't always a jail cell.

- How did/does persecution backfire and actually spread Christianity?

Look into the ministries of some modern-day Pauls.

- Who are they?

- Where and how do they live?

- What kind of work do they do?

- How do they get paid?

- Would you like to go with them sometime? You can! Check it out! See the following Endnotes for contact information of these modern-day apostles.

Note: This text has been influenced by passages in these chapters in the Bible—Acts 8–9; Acts 23; 2 Corinthians 12.

ENDNOTES

1. Leif Hetland, Global Mission Awareness, www
    .globalmissionawareness.com.

2. Heidi Baker, Iris Global, www.irismin.org; *Compelled by Love*
    by Heidi Baker (Charisma House, 2008), 61.

3. Jackie Pullinger, St. Stephen's Society; www.ststephenssociety
    .com.

PHILIP

Philip, however, appeared at Azotus and traveled about, preaching the gospel in all the towns until he reached Caesarea (Acts 8:40).

P hilip was one of those twelve inner-circle apostles who had received the extra lessons and private teachings from Jesus during the last three years of His life. On the rare occasions when Jesus was hanging out with just these twelve guys, they loved to ask Jesus to explain His teachings in greater detail. When I am reading the Bible, sometimes I'll encounter sections that seem unclear to me. It would be so cool to say to Jesus, "What the heck is that supposed mean?" Really, the truth is, I do it anyway. I simply ask God to help me understand the part I am trying to decipher. What does it mean? How can I apply it to my life? Why would God want these particular words in the Bible in the first place? Usually that works out pretty well. I'll get some interesting thoughts pretty quickly.

Sometimes I ask other people what they think about certain verses to get even more perspective. Some folks call the Bible the

"Living Word." It has the capability to say different things to diverse people, and to communicate a shifting message depending on what a person is going through. Having led Bible studies for a number of years now, I get a kick out of comparing what the Bible has spoken to the other people in a discussion group. Brook and I like to leave room for rockin' and rollicking conversations centered on the Word of God. Atheists would probably be amazed at the things we end up discussing in our Bible studies, and would probably enjoy many of these interactions. You see, the Word of God is relevant to every life situation.

Philip is about to help clarify a few things for a man who has questions that he didn't even know he wanted to ask. God knew this guy had questions and has sent Philip to bring the answers. This is how it goes: An angel came to Philip and told him to go on an adventure, a treasure hunt of sorts.[1] The angel suggested that Philip head toward the country road that leads from Jerusalem toward Gaza. (I wonder if that road is still there? I bet it is.) As Philip traveled along, he met a man from Ethiopia. It turns out that this guy was the Ethiopian queen's minister of finance. In my limited way of thinking, my first guess would not have been that an Ethiopian would be Jewish. But, it seems he was. It turns out that there is a faithful Jewish population in Ethiopia even today, thought to be a consequence of the time that the Queen of Sheba spent with King Solomon. This man whom Philip encountered had gone on a pilgrimage to Jerusalem to worship God. As he was heading home, he was sitting in his chariot reading the book of Isaiah in the Hebrew Bible. (The Hebrew Bible, the Tanakh, is the first part of the Christian Bible. Christians call that part the Old Testament.)

The Holy Spirit told Philip to stay close to this guy for a little while. Philip was close enough to hear what the Ethiopian was reading. Philip asked him if he understood what he was reading.

I like the Ethiopian's response. He wasn't defensive or afraid of sounding stupid. He simply said, "How can I understand it unless someone explains it to me?"

Frankly, I am actually a little bit jealous of this reaction! I might have been afraid of looking stupid, trying to hide what I don't know. Or I might have thought, *I understand the thing plenty well and don't need any extra insight, thankyouverymuch.* But I must bear in mind that there is usually more and deeper wisdom to be accessed. This Ethiopian is smarter than me. His humble teachability is something I would like to apply to my own Bible education from this 40 story series. Dude, don't think I'm just writing these things for your benefit! I'm getting a lot out of this labor of love.

Back to it. The Ethiopian asks Philip to sit with him and to share some insights. They start with the very section of Isaiah which the Ethiopian had been contemplating: The Lamb of God being taken to slaughter, deprived of justice in the courts of law, killed, and left with no descendants. The Ethiopian wanted to know what these verses were talking about. Well, who better to ask than one who had been there for the slaughter of Jesus, the true Lamb of God? Philip told him the whole story.

The Ethiopian drank up this information like someone who had been stuck in the desert without a canteen. While he listened to Philip's account of Jesus, the Ethiopian understood his own need for the salvation offered by this spotless Lamb talked about in the writings of Isaiah. He realized that he had been carrying around a bundle of guilty feelings and secret frustrations from which he could never quite get free. But that weight had just lifted. Philip's words also revealed that when people accept Jesus as their Lord and Savior, the next step is baptism. The Ethiopian was so fired up that he wanted to be baptized right away. He was ready to drown his old ways and start brand-new, and he didn't want to wait. By and by, as they traveled along, they came upon a body of water, probably an oasis, since they were on a desert route. The Ethiopian turned to Philip spontaneously and said, "HEY! Why shouldn't I be baptized right now?!" Then he brought the chariot to a screeching halt. Philip and the Ethiopian walked down to the water together and had their own impromptu baptism ceremony.

Here is the mysterious part that people explain in many different ways. When the Ethiopian came out of the waters of baptism, he was alone. Philip was gone. The Spirit of the Lord took Philip away to a whole other place. He was kinda "holy tele-ported" to his next assignment for God, which was on the road to Caesarea. The Ethiopian looked around for Philip, shrugged, and then went on his merry way. There was no tension in this mystery for him. It doesn't even sound like he was all that surprised. The whole situation had been naturally supernatural. He was psyched to have had this great experience. He was reveling in revelation, free from burden, and squeaky clean. Now, he was on his way to share the Good News and his testimony with the very queen of Ethiopia, taking the message of Jesus deeper into Africa. I have learned from one of my proofreaders that the Coptic Monks of Ethiopia were largely responsible for preserving much of the ancient Old and New Testament writings. Perhaps this Ethiopian was the very first Coptic Christian, adding extra value to Philip's assignment to reach this man!

THOUGHTS AND QUESTIONS FOR CONTEMPLATION AND DISCUSSION

Make sure to ask God to speak to you while you read the Bible, and to help you understand.

- How clear is the Bible to you?
- How and why does it help to ask God to speak to you when you read His Word?

- How could the Bible communicate something different to you depending on your circumstances on any given day?

- Do you ever have discussions with others about what different sections might mean?

Open the Bible and look at the table of contents. Which chapters have you heard of? See if you can find some of them! Explore the Bible, reading verses you may never have seen before. If you read the Bible frequently, try reading in a section where you don't usually go. Look for buried treasure!

- How can a person have questions that they don't even know they have?

- Have you ever heard the expression, "They have a God-shaped hole in their heart"? What does that mean?

- What is a treasure hunt as it pertains to this chapter?

- What was the treasure on this treasure map?

- How far-reaching is God's treasure hunt? (There is a book on this topic recommended at the end of this chapter. It is one of my top favorite books.)

- Have you ever felt like you are "supposed to" go talk to somebody? What do you do in that situation?

- What happens when you do, or don't? How does that make you feel?

- How significant is it that this Ethiopian man has a close and trusted relationship with the queen?

- What kind of influence can the Ethiopian have with the queen?

- What close and trusted relationships do you have? Have you ever wondered why?

- How open are you to learning new things?

- What is the value of humble teachability?

- How can you put yourself into an environment where you can access more information without being intimidated?

- Have you ever experienced a hunger or thirst for God?

- What parts of you seem to want a relationship with Him? Mind? Soul? Heart? Physical senses?

- Why did the Ethiopian want to be baptized?

- What does it mean to be baptized?

- Have you ever been baptized?

- Is this a choice you make for yourself, or that others make for you?

- What happened to Philip? How did he disappear?

- The Bible talks about believers taking the message of Jesus to the ends of the earth. What part of this did Philip do?

- What about the queen of Ethiopia, what is her next step? (I looked this up online: As of 2014, Ethiopia is 62 percent Christian.)

- What about you? What part are you supposed to play in taking the message of Jesus to the ends of the earth? Make sure to be asking God from time to time for His opinion on this.

Note: This text has been influenced by Acts 8:26-40 and Isaiah 53:7-8

ENDNOTE

1. *The Ultimate Treasure Hunt* by Kevin Dedmon (Shippensburg, PA: Destiny Image Publishers, 2007). This is one of my top favorite books!

PETER AND TABITHA

Peter sent them all out of the room; then he got down on his knees and prayed. Turning toward the dead woman, he said, "Tabitha, get up." She opened her eyes, and seeing Peter she sat up (Acts 9:40).

You already have the bottom line of this story right up there in the "40 verse" quoted above. Let me give you the background of the biblical time period we are in at this moment. Jesus has died, been raised from the dead, and has come back to visit His friends on earth for 40 days. He has given His followers the Great Commission. Jesus has now ascended to Heaven and has sent His Holy Spirit to live in the believers who choose to accept His invitation to host the Power of God. Peter and John have gone out in the streets talking to people about Jesus, performing miraculous wonders, and getting themselves arrested for it. Steven has been martyred. Saul, not yet Paul, is breathing murderous threats against the Christians. Consequently, the Christians are praying that they will be bolder and have greater power in their representation of Jesus. The Christians are scattering and moving great distances to stay alive. Meanwhile, they tell people in all the world what they have learned about Jesus, God, and the Holy Spirit.

Peter has earned quite a reputation for being a powerful man of God. Peter is the character in the Bible whose mouth used to be slightly larger than his feet. We know this because he was caught putting his feet (yup, both of them) in his mouth a few times. (I can tell you my mouth size has to be at least 7½ . I seem to have been able to get my whole foot in my mouth, plus a big furry boot on a few occasions. I don't mean to sound like I'm bragging either. This is not one of my better qualities. One potentially obtainable goal of mine is to lose my ability to measure my mouth in terms of my shoe size. The godly opposite of this "foot-in-mouth-disease" is that there might be an amazing public speaker hidden somewhere inside me. Watch Peter's progress.)

Peter is becoming one of my favorite Bible heroes! He has learned and grown so much since Jesus rose from the dead. God has entrusted Peter with a lot of responsibility since those foot-in-mouth days of the past. He has proven to be trustworthy and reliable. God started by giving Peter a little bit of freedom and power. Then He'd watch and see what Peter would do with it. Peter wasn't trying to see what he could get away with. Peter was no longer acting out of impulse. Now in this new maturity mode, God was giving him bigger assignments, and Peter kept getting responsibility raises.

By this point, Peter was walking into towns with the Holy Spirit, and these towns would be changed by the time he left. He came to a place called Lydda and had an encounter with a paralyzed guy who had been stuck in his bed for eight years. (It's a good thing my husband, Brook, gets his turn in a chair during this current boon in wheelchair technology. And you should see his bike! I can't imagine my active husband stuck in a bed for eight years. Of course, our plan is to pray him right out of the wheelchair. We sure are going for it, every day.) So Peter meets this guy named Aeneas. (Not one of the popular names from the Bible, eh-hmmm. I'm not actually sure how it is pronounced, but my guess makes it sounds kinda bad.) For Peter it is simple; he says, "Jesus Christ heals you...get up." Sure 'nough, Aeneas stands up. He must have been pretty well known. Literally everyone in that town and the town next to it become Christians just based on that one miracle.

A few towns away, in Joppa, there lived a woman named Tabitha. She was a sweetheart. Everyone loved her. She was always doing kind things for people and helping the poor with her warm heart full of loving compassion. Out of nowhere, she became sick and died quite suddenly. Word had reached Joppa that Peter was nearby in Lydda. Two men went to Peter to tell him about Tabitha's death. Peter came at once. When he got to Joppa, he was taken to see the body. There were some women crying and mourning her death. They showed Peter a bunch of projects that Tabitha had been working on. Oh how industrious she had been...her life cut short. What a theft of life.

Peter sent the mourners out of the room. He got down on his knees and prayed. He wasn't praying for the dead woman. He was talking with God. He was getting himself filled up with the presence and power of God and the Holy Spirit. When he had finished praying, he turned toward the body and said, "Tabitha, get up!" Peter didn't stand there bargaining with God, asking God to come down to earth and fix things. Rather, with the power and authority of the Holy Spirit of Jesus living in him and flowing through him, Peter simply commanded the woman to get up—and she did! She opened her eyes, made eye contact with Peter, and then sat up, *alive.* He called the others back into the room. It doesn't say what happened next, but I bet people were freaking out! Peter stayed in Joppa for a while. Many people in that town came to believe that Jesus is Lord.

It seems to me that God wants more of us to go in the direction Peter went—graduating from a foot muncher to a proactive citizen of the Kingdom of God. I don't think we need to do it in exactly the same way. We don't have to *be* Peter clones. But we should keep moving forward steadily with God, learning about our identity in God, and chasing our destiny with Him. Jesus basically told us to *go* into all the world and make disciples of all nations, teaching them to heal the sick, raise the dead, cast out demons, and cleanse the lepers. Well, what are we waiting for? It certainly won't happen if we never try! Go!

THOUGHTS AND QUESTIONS FOR CONTEMPLATION AND DISCUSSION

- What are your thoughts on Jesus's invitation to host the Power of God, the Holy Spirit?

- How can and do people host the Power of God?

- Have you done this yet?

- Are you intrigued?

- Would you like to be bolder and have greater power in your representation of Jesus? In which parts of your life?

- About foot size and mouth size: Well? Do you know your mouth size? Can you change it?

- How can you overcome your foot-in-mouth ways? Be encouraged. It can be done!

- How did Peter grow into a higher level of assignment and responsibility?

- What are some adjustments you might want to (need to) make to grow in stature with God and people?

- How did Peter handle freedom and power?

- What does the next step toward "maturity mode" look like for you?

- Who is Peter with when he is walking into new towns?

- What happens between the time when Peter arrives and leaves these towns?

- Can people die at the wrong time?

- Can life be stolen?

- What is Peter's technique for praying for the sick? (For more information on this prayer style, check out Brian Thompson's course: School of Signs & Wonders, available at www.wagnerleadership .ca. This course will boost your faith and take you to a new level of prayer. Seriously!)

- How do you think you would react to seeing someone being raised from the dead? (It really has to be quite an event!)

- How would that change you and the people you know?

- Have you thought about what you are going to do when you finish this book?

- How well do you understand the great commission?

- Are you feeling as if there is more to Christianity than you had realized?

- Are you ready to go to the next level?

- Have you figured out your current level?

I recommend the following books and film. If you have access to the Internet, you can go to amazon.com and even read the first chapters of some books. You can also read the editorial reviews and customer reviews and ratings. Some of these resources are foundational. (See a complete Recommended Reading list at the end of this book.)

- *Questions of Life: A Practical Introduction to the Christian Faith by Nicky Gumbel* (David C. Cook Publishing Company, 2002).

- *Close Encounters of the Divine Kind* by Che Ahn with Linda M. Radford (Charisma House, 2007).

- *The Supernatural Ways of Royalty: Discovering Your Rights and Privileges of Being a Son or Daughter of God* by Bill Johnson and Kris Vallotton (Destiny Image Publishers, 2006).

- *When Heaven Invades Earth* by Bill Johnson (Destiny Image Publishers, 2005).

- *Finger of God*, DVD film, by Darren Wilson. You really have to check this one out! It's a faith-lifting supernatural movie with miracles filmed in it. Visit the website: http://fingerofgod.wpfilm.com.

Note: This text has been influenced by Acts 9:32-43 in the Bible.

CLOUD OF WITNESSES

God had planned something better for us so that only together with us would they be made perfect (Hebrews 11:40).

As you have been reading these chapters, you have been introduced to "a great cloud of witnesses" (Hebrews 12:1). Many of the people in these stories will be up in Heaven ready to party with us for the rest of eternity. Of course there will be a few of the characters who won't make the cut, like Jezebel. I have to tell you the saddest part of what Jezebel did (in my opinion)—she ruined the best girl name in the Bible! You just can't name a baby girl Jezebel without giving her a tainted label. Oops, once again I have digressed. How about some of the other characters making it to Heaven? I'm not sure. We'll have to wait and see. I have a heart of compassion for Judas, but I'd be really surprised to see him in Heaven. Joash?

Dunno. But, oh to meet David, Moses, and Elijah! And Mary Magdalene—I want to hear her whole story! And apostle Peter! My heart bursts with anticipation.

I gotta tell you something goofy. I met Bill Murray. His public persona was fun and pleasant, he seems quite likable in person. But I was the idiot in the circle who quoted his character from *Caddyshack*. Dulp...DUH! He didn't seem to mind; he's good about being quoted; but I sure felt silly afterward. I guess I can't make a fool out of myself in Heaven, "so at least I've got that going for me!"[1] Seriously, I want to be able to walk up to these biblical heroes and ask them questions—get to know them. I plan on meeting the people we've discussed. To me they aren't just characters in stories. This is eternal history, and I'm part of it.

In the Bible book called Hebrews, chapter 11 is referred to as "The Hall of Faith." This is the Hall of Fame for those full of faith. Faith is mind-boggling. The people mentioned in this chapter are like pillars in the house of God. An interesting thing to note if you would study Hebrews 11 carefully is this: The way God tells the story of someone's life can be different from how the history in a person's life seemed to unfold. The easiest example to relate is the story of Sarah. Sarah was an old, barren woman. All you had to do was look at Sarah and you could see that no babies were going to be coming out of her womb. She was old, dried up, past the age.

God came and talked to Sarah's husband, Abraham, and told him that he and Sarah were going to have a baby. Sarah had been eavesdropping. When she heard this, she laughed. It was not a laugh of joy. You can look in Genesis 18:12 to read how it really went down. It was a scoff, a laugh of mockery and unbelief. But, if you read in Hebrews 11, you can see that God re-wrote the story. It says Sarah had faith in God's promise. My guess is that it didn't take too long for her to stop mocking and start believing. That new version of the story was then written as she changed her way of thinking, renewed her mind. That is the part God remembers. Her reward was that she gave birth to that baby when she was 100 years old. His name was Isaac, which means laughter. Pain and shame were turned into happiness.

And so it can be for you. A great person of faith and joy is being born in your heart; and each day is pregnant with promise, even if *you* think it is too late. God has put the Christians from our time period on the same team as the people in these 40 stories—the ones from the Hall of Faith. You know when you watch the Olympics and they have that relay running race? There are four different runners on a team; one starts out and passes a baton to the next guy...and so on...until all four have run. Well, our generation is still part of a heavenly relay race. Those of us who choose to believe that Jesus is Lord and that what the Bible says is the Truth, we are bringing the baton closer to the finish line. We have to run our best race. I've heard that the best strategy for a relay race is to put the fastest guy as the last runner. In our time, we have to run this race, life on earth with a great commission, like we are the fourth runner on the team.

When we read about Noah, Job, Moses, Joshua, Deborah, Gideon, Samson, David, Solomon, Elijah, Jonah, Isaiah, Jeremiah, Nehemiah, Peter, Paul, Mary, and the rest, we need to keep in mind that the baton has not yet crossed the finish line. None of these people on our team were completely perfect (except Jesus). The Israelites whined. Elijah got scared and suicidal. David and Moses both murdered. Noah got drunk. Sarah mocked God. Peter? He had his foot in his mouth over and over. Paul persecuted Christians to death. Get the picture? However, when these people had the things of God in their hearts, they ran from victory toward victory. Here is a good question to consider: What happens to the other people on our team if *we* drop the baton?

You know people who need help. You can easily see a world that is overrun by evil. People are angry, despairing, hurting, and sick. People are emotionally paralyzed. We need to go get 'em, grab their hands, give them a gentle tug, encourage them to stand up and join the team, and start running.

Let God rewrite your story. We need you on the team. On your mark, get set, GO! Seek God with all your heart and He will give you a future custom-made just for *you,* for just exactly the you He created you to be.

Jeremiah 29:11-13 says:

> *"I know the plans I have for you," declares the Lord, "plans to prosper you and not to harm you, plans to give you hope and a future. Then you will call upon me and come and pray to me, and I will listen to you. You will seek me and find me when you seek me with all your heart."*

THOUGHTS AND QUESTIONS FOR CONTEMPLATION AND DISCUSSION

- Which of the people in these 40 stories are you looking forward to meeting in Heaven? Why?

- Who else?

- How have some of the characters in the Bible become more real to you as you have been going through these chapters?

- How can God rewrite history, making it "His story"?

- Does He change it?

- From what perspective is He looking when He looks at our history?

- What parts of your life are you hoping God rewrites?

- What characteristics would you like to be listed after your name in God's book?

- How does a relay race work?

- How does your performance affect the race?

- What happens to the people on your team if you drop the baton?

- How does this "relay race" metaphor work if you are the third or fourth runner?

- When you look at the list of things that some of these "pillars" did wrong along the way, how does that encourage you to move forward in your part of the race?

- How can God use people who have made such serious mistakes? He does this a lot. Why does He do this?

- What does it mean to drop the baton?

- Will God choose someone else to do the assignment that you were supposed to do if you decide you don't feel like doing that task?

- Is it possible that you were supposed to rescue someone, but you walked on by, and now they will never receive their recovery, salvation, or healing?

- Beyond being shy and in a hurry, what lifestyles and attitudes are blocking you from _____?

- What do you suppose it might mean to run "from victory toward victory"?

- What is victory?

- Followers of Jesus are positioned in victory. How does that affect your ability to complete the tasks God had planned for you?

- Think of people you know who have difficulties. How can you help those who are angry, despairing, hurting, sick, and emotionally paralyzed?

- What happens to you as you minister to others?

- According to Jeremiah 29:11-13, what are God's plans for *you?*

Note: This text has been influenced by these chapters in the Bible—Hebrews 11; Genesis 18 and 21.

ENDNOTE

1. Woohoo, I managed to get a *Caddyshack* quote in there! That's from Bill Murray's character talking about his visit with the Dalai Lama: "Gunga la gunga!" *Caddyshack,* director Harold Ramis, Warner Brothers, 1980.

PART VII

NOW—YOUR TURN

"CHAPTER 40"

Ah-ha, I have found a 40 loophole! Isn't it part of human nature to keep an eye out for the loophole? Gotta love a legitimate loophole. Because this is "Chapter 40," I can write about anything I want! I don't have to seek out a story, a verse, or a chapter with the number 40 in it. Holy guacamole, Dude, can you believe we've done 40 of these things? Awesome! God has been so good to us!

So, here's my plan for Chapter 40:

1. I suggest that you reread these 40 stories. There is a *lot* of information in these chapters. If you haven't fully absorbed them, then there is still stuff for you to soak up. Put it this way, there is still stuff for me to absorb, and I'm the one who wrote 40 letters, then turned them into 40 chapters, then compiled a bunch of mind-crunching questions to go with them, and proofread the whole shebang multiple times. You might be amazed at how much more stuff there is for you in these fortifications. (I can't believe it myself. I've really surprised myself here.) Plus, people might ask you big life questions, and I suspect you'll want to have some good answers.

2. Look into the books, websites, and other resources list-
    ed at the end of these chapters. The content in this book
    should have stirred up a lot more questions for you. It
    should be a lifelong pursuit to keep finding answers.
    God has arranged an Easter egg hunt of great mystery
    for us to seek out His treasures. The better we get at
    finding eggs, the better He hides the next one. God is
    really having a lot of fun as we hunt and find revelation
    hidden for us, not from us.

3. I urge you to reassess the Good News and even the
    warnings included in these stories. As you do this, ask
    God to release your destiny to you. Ask Him what it is
    that He created you to do. He has made *you* uniquely
    fascinating. The enemy of your soul has tried to get you
    to think that those marvelous quirks of yours are flaws,
    and that you don't qualify to introduce Heaven every-
    where you tread. *But,* we know now that satan is a liar…
    that all bad things come from him. You were made to
    rock! Remember that God has a plan to *prosper* you, to
    give you *hope* and a *good future.* Generally speaking, you
    won't get your complete assignment from God until you
    are in alignment with Him. It is beneficial to pursue that
    alignment, so you can be released to the assignment.

4. Now I am going to ask you to consider becoming
    Christian, or to rededicate your life to God. I'm not go-
    ing to pressure you. This is a big life decision, and quite
    personal. I'm simply providing you with information
    and a framework. I have written a prayer that you can
    read through and contemplate. Yup, you can pray about
    praying this prayer. Or, you can take the smartest risk
    of your life and just go for it. Choosing a Higher Power

is important. ("Crucial" would be a better word. Notice "crucial" has something in common with the word "crucifix," the cross on which Jesus died.) It would be a mistake to choose a Higher Power that is a counterfeit or has no power or is lower than the Highest Power. Choose wisely!

What follows is a rough outline of a prayer to ask the Holy Trinity (God, Jesus, and the Holy Spirit) to become activated in your life. Of course I have written it in a way that I talk to God, so you can change the words and say it in your own way. God likes that.

Lord, I have to confess, I've made more than my fair share of mistakes and bad decisions. I have hurt people's feelings, and I bet I have disappointed You, and hurt You, too. I ask that You would forgive me, and give me a fresh start to do life better and better each new day. Lord, I have enjoyed these 40 stories. I have learned things about You and Your nature that I never knew. Other stuff I had forgotten or ignored and not applied to my life. Now I want to know You more. You have my attention. Come into my life and guide me into wondrous possibilities. Teach me more amazing things about You, and about me, too. Reveal to me who You created me to be. Unlock my destiny so that I can have the rich and full life that You planned for me. Come live in my heart and my mind. I invite You to be part of my life—Father, Spirit, and Son. Take my mess and turn it into a message! Take my tests and forge them into a testimony. I forgive and release anyone who has hurt me—including myself! And Lord? What can I do for You? (Listen for God at this point in the prayer. Let Him give you a fresh thought.) *I pray these things in Jesus's power and character, amen.*

And, don't let a bad day, a bad minute, or a bad whatever get in your way and block your future with God. He loves you. You are His child. He always wants you to come to Him, no matter what.

THOUGHTS AND QUESTIONS FOR CONTEMPLATION AND DISCUSSION

- How many times do you think you would have to read the Bible to understand every "application" for your life?

- Do you think that it's possible to understand everything in the Bible? (Each time, before you begin to read the Bible, ask the Holy Spirit of God to open your eyes, ears, mind, and heart to what God Himself wants you to learn. It's amazing how much more you will understand when you ask the Holy Spirit to help you.)

- Have you ever noticed the way that a Bible verse, or even a story adapts and changes to fit the situation you are in? (If not yet, look for this in your future.) Explain why the Bible is also called the "Living Word."

- How is studying God and His mysteries like an Easter egg hunt? Think about the scenario of an Easter egg hunt and the joy it brings children *and* grown-ups.

- How has this book answered some of your life questions?

- How has it raised more questions?

- How has this increased your interest in God, Jesus, and the Holy Spirit?

- What new aspects about your destiny are you learning these days?

- Has something totally unexpected happened, or have you known most of this stuff all along?

- Do you feel more hopeful, brave, and better equipped to head toward your destiny?

- What parts of your life are still not in alignment with your assignment?

- How are you planning to progress through those blockades?

- In choosing a Higher Power, what are the risks?

- What is a counterfeit, and a lower power? What do these others do? How can you identify them?

- Why is it important to get to know the complete Holy Trinity (God, Jesus, and the Holy Spirit)?

- How do they fit together as One God? (P.S. If you can answer this set of questions, it's your turn to write a book! Ha! It is good to contemplate things bigger than we can grasp. It puts a perspective on how superlative God is.)

- What parts of the salvation prayer touched your heart and soul the most?

- Do you find it easy to talk to God in your own words?

- Do you feel like you have to use special language, like in Shakespeare plays, or be hyper-polite and formal, or can you easily be yourself?

- When you listened for God to give you a fresh thought, what happened? If you are not sure you heard something, don't stop listening. It might take a little bit of time to understand how God speaks to you. He doesn't always reveal Himself with words alone. Use all of your senses.

- What are you going to do if you have a bad day, or even a bad minute?

OK, now what? What are you going to do next to keep seeking God? I'm serious! You've got to keep this ball rolling! Now, *go git'er dun!*

140 NAMES OF GOD

I had started out on a hunt for 40 Names of God. Then I found over 65, so I decided to make two chapters, 40 and 40 more. Then it grew to three chapters, with 40 More Again. But, I would have to cut some because there were too many. Then I realized I could easily find enough to make 140, so that is what I did. There are still many more names of God that I skipped. That is to say, this is an incomplete list of the names of God. As you read through the list, see which names pop out at you. This could be another hint for moving toward your destiny. Who is God to *you?* I have heard it taught: Who God is *to* you, He would like to be *through* you.

ALMIGHTY	*Advocate*	Cornerstone
Adonai	Author of Eternal Salvation	CARPENTER
ABBA FATHER	BELOVED SON	Creator
Alpha & Omega	Bread of Life	Consuming Fire
Ancient of Days	BRIDEGROOM	Comforter
Author of Life	CHRIST	Counselor

Crown of Glory

Covenant Deliverer

Desire of All Nations

Door

Dayspring

Elohim

El Shaddai

Eternal Life

EVERLASTING GOD

Father

Father of the Fatherless

Faithful & True

Firstborn of Many Brethren

Foundation

FRIEND

FORTRESS

FOUNTAIN

Gentle Whisper

God

God of All Comfort

God of Grace

GOD OF GODS

God of the Living

Guide

God Who Sees Me

GREAT HIGH PRIEST

Great Reward

He in Whom I Trust

HE WHO JUDGES ME

Holy Spirit

Holy Ghost

Hiding Place

Holy One of God

Heir of All Things

Head of the Body

Horn of Salvation

Hope

Healer

I AM

IMAGE OF GOD

JEHOVAH

JESUS

Judge

King of the Jews

King of Glory

KING OF KINGS

KING OF HEAVEN

Life

Lamb of God

LAST ADAM

Leader

Lord of All

Lion of Judah

LIVING STONE

Light of the World

Love

LIVING WATER

LORD

Lord of Hosts

Lord of Glory

Lord of lords

Lover of My Soul

Messiah

Master

Morning Star

MIGHTY ONE OF ISRAEL

Majesty

Messenger

Merciful God

Mediator

My Beloved

Nazarene

Oil of Gladness

Our Passover Lamb

Our Father

PRINCE OF PEACE

STRENGTH OF MY HEART

SHALOM

STAR OUT OF JACOB

True Vine

TEACHER

PROMISE OF THE FATHER

Potter

Redeemer

Rabbi

REFUGE

RESURRECTION

Righteous One

RULER OF KINGS

Rock

Ransom

River of Life

ROSE OF SHARON

Savior

SALVATION

Son of Man

THREE IN ONE

The Amen

The Breaker

The Godhead

The Way, The Truth, The Life

Shepherd

Seed

Second Adam

Sanctuary

Son of God

SON OF DAVID

Spirit of Christ

Shield

Servant

Spirit of Revelation

Spirit of Wisdom

Stone

Shelter

Sun of Righteousness

Strong Tower

Wisdom of God

Wonderful Counselor

Word of Life

YAHWEH

Your Maker

RECOMMENDED
RESOURCES

Always Enough: God's Miraculous Provision among the Poorest Children on Earth by Heidi Baker. Ada, MI: Chosen, 2003.

Basic Training for the Prophetic Ministry by Kris Vallotton. Shippensburg, PA: Destiny Image, 2007.

Close Encounters of the Divine Kind by Che Ahn with Linda M. Radford. Lake Mary, FL: Charisma House, 2007.

Compelled by Love: How to Change the World through the Simple Power of Love in Action by Heidi Baker. Lake Mary, FL: Charisma House, 2008.

Face to Face with God by Bill Johnson. Lake Mary, FL: Charisma House, 2007.

Father Loves You, a CD teaching on God's love by Leif Hetland. I heartily recommend all teachings by Leif Hetland; his other books, CDs, and DVDs are amazing, too. Visit the online bookstore at the Global Mission Awareness: www .globalmissionawareness.com.

Finger of God, DVD Film by Darren Wilson. You have to check this one out! It's a faith-lifting supernatural movie with filmed miracles. Visit http://fingerofgod.wpfilm.com. Darren Wilson has made other films, too. Good stuff!

Heal Them All by Cheryl Schang. Xulon Press, 2005.

Love Stains by Bob Johnson. Red Arrow Publishing, 2013.

Questions of Life: A Practical Introduction to the Christian Faith by Nicky Gumbel. Colorado Springs, CO: David C. Cook Publishing Company, 2002.

Rebuilding the Real You: The Definitive Guide to the Holy Spirit's Work in Your Life by Jack Hayford. Lake Mary, FL: Charisma House, 2009.

Spirit Formed, The Nehemiah Series by Dr. Jack Hayford. Available online at https://www.jackhayford.org/store/nehemiah-pictures-of-the-holy-spirit/.

The School of Seers Expanded Edition: A Practical Guide on How to See in the Unseen Realm by Jonathan Welton. Shippensburg, PA: Destiny Image Publishers, 2013.

The Supernatural Power of a Transformed Mind: Access to a Life of Miracles by Bill Johnson. Shippensburg, PA: Destiny Image Publishers, 2005. This book changed the direction of my life. It is a "spiritual filet mignon."

The Supernatural Ways of Royalty: Discovering Your Rights and Privileges of Being a Son or Daughter of God by Bill Johnson and Kris Vallotton. Shippensburg, PA: Destiny Image Publishers, 2006.

The Ultimate Treasure Hunt by Kevin Dedmon. Shippensburg, PA: Destiny Image Publishers, 2007.

User Friendly Prophecy by Larry Randolph. Shippensburg, PA: Destiny Image Publishers, 1998.

When Heaven Invades Earth by Bill Johnson. Shippensburg, PA: Destiny Image Publishers, 2005.

MINISTRIES MAKING A
DIFFERENCE WORLDWIDE

Heidi Baker, Iris Global; www.irismin.org.

Randy Clark's Healing Schools; also, Voice of the Apostles Conference, Global Awakening, Phone: 866-AWAKENING (866-292-5364), www.globalawakening.com.

Jackie Pullinger, St. Stephen's Society; www.ststephenssociety.com.

Caron Foundation, Comprehensive Drug & Alcohol Addiction Treatment Center; www.caron.org, or call the 24-hour hotline: 800-854-6023.

Teen Challenge provides care for adults and adolescents who need intensive help with life-controlling problems: www .teenchallengeusa.com.

Betel International is a great place to make a clean start; amazing recovery record with programs and communities in more than 20 nations: http://betelinternational.org.

BIBLES ON YOUR COMPUTER/PHONE APPS

www.biblegateway.com—offers many versions of the Bible.

www.accordancebible.com—comprehensive; for basic study and reading, or grow it into a huge resource with multiple study guides, Greek and Hebrew translation, and tons of maps and pictures.

ABOUT
LAURIE HAYDEN BERGEY

Laurie Hayden Bergey and her husband, Brook, are the founders of Miracle Waters Ministries and The Gift List. Laurie has her Masters in Practical Ministry. She also serves as an ordained deacon at New Covenant Christian Community Church in Bethlehem, PA. Her creative passions include being a glass jewelry master craftsman and an amateur chocolatier. Laurie has also served in the United States Peace Corps in Niger, West Africa.

Visit the author's ministry website: miraclewaters.org.

Visit the author's blog: fortifymylife.wordpress.com